How to
Thrive
From
9 to 5

HOW TO THRIVE FROM 9 TO 5

You Can Do More Than
Just Survive on Your Job

Mary Whelchel

VINE
BOOKS

SERVANT PUBLICATIONS
ANN ARBOR, MICHIGAN

9562034

Vine Books is an imprint of Servant Publications especially designed to serve evangelical Christians.

All Scripture quotations, unless otherwise indicated, are taken from the HOLY BIBLE, NEW INTERNATIONAL VERSION, © 1974, 1978, 1983, and 1984 by the International Bible Society. Used by permission of Zondervan Publishing House. Scripture references indicated KJV are from The King James Version. Scripture references indicated NASB are from the New American Standard Version, copyright © 1960, 1962, 1963, 1968, 1971, 1973, 1975, 1977, the Lockman Foundation. Used by permission.

Published by Servant Publications
P.O. Box 8617
Ann Arbor, Michigan 48107

Cover design: Alan Furst, Minneapolis, Minnesota

99 00 01 02   10 9   8   7   6   5   4   3   2   1

Printed in the United States of America
ISBN 1-56955-169-3

LIBRARY OF CONGRESS CATALOGING-IN-PUBLICATION DATA

Whelchel, Mary.
     How to thrive from 9 to 5 / Mary Whelchel
        p.   cm.
     ISBN 1-56955-169-3 (alk. paper)
     1. Occupational training—Handbooks, manuals, etc.   2. Vocational guid-
ance—Handbooks, manuals, etc.   3. Job satisfaction—Handbooks, manuals,
etc.   I. Title.   II. Title: How to thrive from nine to five.
HD5715.W52   1999
650.1—dc21   99-22886
                                                     CIP

To my brothers, George and Roger Stiles,
who have endured their baby sister
with grace and kindness through many years.
I love and admire you both.

Contents

Take Your Survive/Thrive Temperature!

For over fifteen years I've traveled all over the country, giving business seminars to people from every kind of job and company, on a wide range of topics from customer service, to communicating effectively, to getting along with people. One thing stands out loud and clear from this experience: Most people are just surviving on their jobs. It's a daily battle for them to simply get out of bed and face another day in that office or classroom or plant or hospital or truck or bus—or whatever environment they're in.

I've done my share of surviving, too, and I've learned most of my lessons through failure and experience. I was one of the first women in IBM sales—many years ago—and then moved on into marketing and management positions in IBM and other companies. But much of my career was spent in the survival mode. Finally I realized how foolish that was and started learning to thrive on my job. It dawned on me that since I have to spend ten hours (or more) a day in that spot, it would be much better to gain and grow from it rather than just trying to live through it.

As I traveled the country making these presentations, my desire was to help others catch that very simple but extremely important vision: Your job can be a growing, thriving place if you will learn and practice some basic principles and disciplines. Even in the midst of problems, difficult people, unpleasant working environments, too much work, etc., we have the opportunity to turn negative situations into personal class-rooms, where we use them as a means of growth and maturity. A *thriver* is a person who learns to turn pain into gain.

I wrote this book as a simple but practical aid to the reader who has the desire to be a thriver. I have included many examples from the lives of survivors and thrivers I know. Their stories are true, but I have changed the names to protect their privacy.

This book may contain nothing terribly new to you; the things that produce thrivers today are the same as they've always been. But if you need a refresher course, if you've been a little discouraged lately about your job, if you've wanted to give up and give in too often lately, whether you work from nine to five or eight to six, this book is for you.

How to Use This Book

This book can be used in many different ways for different purposes:

1. To help individuals find practical ways to identify the *survival* areas in their lives and turn them into *thriving* areas
2. To help managers and supervisors deal more successfully with their employees
3. As a manual for training sessions
4. As a reference and handbook on practical skills required in our daily work

Each chapter ends with an exercise to help you in the application of the principles and skills covered by that chapter. The exercises are intended to make the topic more relevant and practical and can be used in training sessions or by individuals.

The book can be read or studied in part or whole and in any sequence that you desire. Each chapter stands alone on a single topic, and some chapters may be more applicable to your situation than others.

In many chapters you will find quotations from the book of Proverbs in the Bible. I find it to be one of the most practical books in helping me with everyday situations on the job and dealing with people. I encourage you to read it often. There are thirty-one chapters, so it is easy to read one chapter a day, corresponding to the day of the month.

In Proverbs 14:23 we read, "All hard work brings a profit, but mere talk leads only to poverty." If you only talk read about thriving on your job, it will lead you to lower levels than you are now. Talk alone doesn't make anything happen.

This book is designed for action, with questions, exercises, and suggestions that you can incorporate into your daily routine and skills. It will require some hard work, but that hard work will bring a great profit for you and for the kingdom of Christ.

Jesus said, "Now that you know these things, you will be blessed if you do them" (Jn 13:17). I hope you will not be a hearer or reader only, but a doer! That's when you reap the blessings.

Before reading this book, take the following self-test to see where you are on the thrive/survive scale.

If I can help you in any way, please write to me:

Mary Whelchel
Box 441
Wheaton, IL 60189

Your Thrive/Survive Self-Test

Find out if you're thriving on your job or just surviving. Answer the following questions as honestly as you can, checking all that apply.

1. Which of these terms describe your attitude toward your job?
   - ☐ boring
   - ☐ beneath me
   - ☐ too much work
   - ☑ stressful
   - ☑ hectic
   - ☐ constant crisis

2. Which of these things are typical of what you think or say about your job?
   - ☐ "I hate this job."
   - ☐ "I can never get along with _____."
   - ☑ "It's Monday (or some other day); Mondays are always terrible!"
   - ☑ "I'll never get my work done on time."
   - ☑ "I'll be glad when this day/week is over."
   - ☑ "If he/she says that to me one more time, I'll scream!"

3. Which of these describe your analysis of your immediate manager(s)?
   - ☑ incompetent
   - ☐ unappreciative
   - ☑ nonsupportive
   - ☑ poor communicator
   - ☑ poor listener
   - ☑ disorganized

4. Which of the following types of conversations do you frequently have with your coworkers?
- ☑ complain about the work environment
- ☐ gossip about coworkers
- ☑ gripe about pay
- ☑ bad-mouth managers
- ☑ complain about the work load
- ☑ criticize management decisions or system

5. Which of the following have you done more than once in the past three weeks?
- ☐ arrived late for work
- ☐ turned in assignments late or miss deadlines often
- ☐ taken long lunch hours
- ☐ made too many personal telephone calls at work
- ☑ left your work station unattended to chat with others

6. Which of the following have you done in the last three months?
- ☐ asked your manager for performance feedback
- ☐ offered to help a coworker who had a heavy work load
- ☐ did something for a customer that you did not have to do
- ☑ got to work early or stayed late for a special project or heavy work load situation

7. Which of the following skills have you tried to acquire or improve in the last six months?
- ☐ telephone manners
- ☐ listening skills
- ☐ dealing with angry people
- ☐ professional appearance
- ☑ body language

8. What professional development have you pursued, either formally or informally, in the last six months?
- ☑ software education
- ☑ computer education
- ☐ presentation skills
- ☐ time-management skills
- ☑ other job-related education

9. Which of the following have you ever done?
- ☑ asked for more responsibility
- ☑ suggested a better system to give more efficient service
- ☐ proposed a rewrite of your job description
- ☑ asked for a training session
- ☑ checked out local opportunities for furthering your education and skills

10. Which of the following do you practice?
- ☑ return phone calls promptly
- ☑ keep track of and follow up on every commitment and promise made and every responsibility accepted
- ☑ compliment others who do a good job
- ☑ ask coworkers for advice and comments when appropriate

How to Score Yourself

Questions 1 through 5:
For every answer *not* checked, give yourself 5 points.

Questions 6 through 10:
For every answer checked, give yourself 5 points.

Total Points

0–20 Not even surviving; on your last leg!

21–75 Barely surviving.

76–110 Surviving with good and bad days—more bad than good!

111–170 Better than just surviving; you thrive on occasion.

171–200 You're a thriver most of the time.

201–260 You're growing and thriving all the time. Congratulations!

Chapter One

It's Time for an Attitude Checkup

"**I** know he won't give me the raise he promised," Elaine said to me, telling me of her upcoming appraisal. "I've worked so hard for this company and gone beyond the call of duty time and again. You'd think he could at least come through with a decent raise."

"How do you know he won't give you a raise?" I asked.

"Oh, I just know the way he is," Elaine responded. "He says those things just to string you along, but when push comes to shove, he doesn't deliver."

"You mean he has promised you raises before and then failed to give them?" I probed further.

"Well, no, not exactly, but I just know he won't come through. He'll find some excuse to put it off—or he'll just ignore it altogether. I'll never get that raise."

With those negative words, Elaine set herself up for failure. Why? Because her attitude was so rotten, it would undoubtedly affect her performance, which indeed could lead to a self-fulfilling prophecy: Elaine wouldn't get the raise she wanted. Who wants to give a raise to someone who looks sour all day, never says anything pleasant, and has a chip on her shoulder?

A bad attitude will guarantee that you'll never do more than just survive on your job. You'll just get by, dragging in and out each day, feeling put-upon and wallowing in self-pity.

Attitude can be defined as how you think in your heart, and the Bible teaches us that as we think in our hearts, so we are (Prv 23:7, NASB).

How you think in your heart about your job, your boss, your coworkers, yourself, your contribution, your company—all of these are part of your overall attitude. If you and I are going to thrive on our jobs, we're going to have to develop and maintain the right attitude.

Unfortunately, attitude cannot be taught. There is no formula for it, no magical dust, no ten-step plan guaranteed to give you the right attitude. Attitude can be learned, but only by people who determine to teach themselves and who realize it has to be learned and relearned daily! It's a lifelong process.

What Is Your Attitude Reputation?

If we surveyed people who know you really well—those who live with you and work with you—how would they describe you? Mostly positive? Mostly negative? Half and half? Did you ever think about your attitude reputation? You have one, whether you realize it or not, and it is very important for us to be aware of exactly where we are on the attitude scale. Generally we fall into one of three attitude categories shown below.

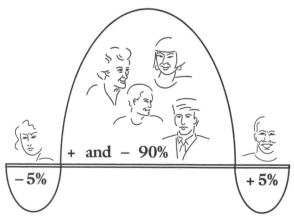

+ and − 90%

−5%   +5%

First, you have two small extremes—the plus-five percenters and the minus-five percenters. Did you ever know a plus-five percenter? He or she smiles all the time and loves everybody and never complains about anything. Now, I'm not sure plus-five percenters breathe the same air you and I do, and they may live in denial at times, but they're a lot nicer to be around than minus-five percenters. You've known some of those, haven't you? They gripe about everything. They never have anything nice to say about anybody. The weather never suits them. They always feel bad, etc.

However, few of us are totally positive or totally negative. Most of us fit in the middle 90 percent somewhere. We're both positive and negative. We have good days and bad days, up times and down times. However, you can be on the plus or minus end of that scale. In other words, you may be more positive than negative or more negative than positive.

Now, think very candidly: Where would you place yourself on the attitude scale on a typical day? Would you honestly be able to say you're a 70 to 80 percent positive person? Or would you have to say you're probably more like half and half?

Maybe some of you would even have to admit that all too often your thoughts are in negative territory and you tend to be more negative than positive. You think too much about the bad things that might happen or have happened, or you imagine the worst. Or you tell yourself it's going to be a bad day or you'll never get your work all done. Or you tell yourself you just can't get along with somebody—or some other negative message that you feed into your head throughout the day.

Your Attitude Is Always Your Choice

I hope you will remember this: Your attitude is your choice. It always is. We live in an age that has developed the art of shifting blame to very high levels, and sometimes we get caught up in that same tendency. "Well, if you had my job you wouldn't be so positive." "If you had my kids, you wouldn't feel so good." "If only my boss were different, I could be a positive person." In other words, "My bad attitude is not my fault!"

The truth is, however, your attitude and mine are *always* our choice. No matter how bad things are, no one can force you to have a bad attitude if you don't want to, and no matter how good things are, no one can force you to have a good attitude if you don't want to. Now, that should come as really good news because it says our attitudes don't have to be the victims of our circumstances or of other people. *We choose our responses.*

The more you understand that and burn it into your mind, the less stress you will have to deal with. The great news is that as believers in the Lord Jesus Christ, with the power of the Holy Spirit within us, we are not in this by ourselves. We have more than our own positive mental attitude to help us. We have the power of God to enable us to do what otherwise might be difficult or impossible.

Think about where you are in the attitude department, and make it a matter of daily prayer. Ask God to break the power of negative thinking in your life; often Satan gets a real stronghold in our lives that way. It's subtle and hard to recognize at first, but if you're ever going to reduce your stress, you must face your attitude for what it is and start today to make it a serious matter of prayer and commitment that you will think biblically—positively.

Don't let New Age philosophy steal from you a wonderful biblical principle—to think about good and positive things. While it is true that a positive mental attitude will not solve the world's problems (contrary to New Age teaching we are not the masters of our fate through positive thinking), it is also true that when we think the way Philippians 4:8 teaches us to, we will think positively. That verse tells us to think about things that are true, noble, right, pure, lovely, admirable, excellent, or praiseworthy. If that isn't positive, I don't know what is. Don't ever lose this biblical principle of thinking positively.

Learn to Reframe

One technique that may be helpful is called *reframing*. Reframing is taking a bad situation and putting it in a different frame. Learn to give it a different look—focus on what might be positive rather than negative.

Recently Tanya was telling me about her job situation. She works in a stressful situation that has been difficult for her to deal with in the past. Tanya's boss is incompetent and irrational, and she spends lots of time spinning her wheels because of his ineptitude and ego. But she's been learning to reframe him.

Tanya said to me, "I think my boss has changed. It sure seems like he's changed. But maybe it's me that's changed; I'm not sure. At any rate, things are so much better at work now. I get along with him much better than I used to."

Tanya is learning to see her boss through different eyes. She does that through prayer—through God's power enabling her to see her boss as God sees him. If you can learn to do this, it will change your attitude tremendously.

I remember one period of my life when I had to deal with a very difficult boss. For quite a few months all I could see was how terrible he was—how intimidating and condescending. Impossible! I tried to find another job, to run away, and I wanted to blame my attitude problem on him. I thought that as long as I worked for him, I couldn't be expected to have a positive attitude. Finally the Lord showed me that I was not in that job by accident and that he wanted me to learn some valuable lessons there before he moved me on. I spent two more years working for that impossible boss, but God helped me to reframe him—to see him differently.

You can reframe a situation or a person through prayer. That's where it began for me. I began to pray for my boss—not that lightning would strike him, but that God would give me compassion for him, help me to see him as God saw him, to understand him, and to respond to him in wisdom. What a difference that reframing made in my performance, my ability to cope with him, my stress levels, and consequently in my attitude.

I imagine there is someone or something in your life you need to reframe today. Maybe it's your attitude toward your schedule or your duties. Often I find myself thinking, "Oh, I have so much to do. I'll never get this all done." Then I start feeling sorry for myself, which adds a lot to my stress level.

I'm learning to reframe that thought. Instead of thinking of all that I have to do in a negative way, I reframe it and say to myself, "Mary, aren't you blessed to have so much to do? Can you imagine how bored you would be if you had lots of time on your hands? Isn't it incredible that God allows you to be a part of his plan to bless and help others?"

As soon as I reframe that situation, my heart rate goes down, my blood pressure goes down, my teeth unclench, my stress is reduced, and my attitude changes. Reframing is a great technique, and it's all in your mind. Proverbs tells us that as we think in our hearts, so are we. It all begins with your thoughts.

Spend Your Emotional Money
More Carefully

Another technique that I use frequently is to be more frugal about how I spend my emotional money. Let me illustrate this for you. We all have what I call an emotional-mental bank account. Now, it is our responsibility to replenish that account, and we do that through appropriate deposits of sleep, good food, exercise, laughter, support systems, etc. But on any given day, you and I have a certain limited amount of emotional money to spend.

Let's say today I start with fifty dollars in my emotional bank account. Before I even leave home, perhaps I have some heated words with my children or my spouse. (Use your imagination, because I'm single.) "You left your clothes on the bathroom floor again!" Or, "You never help me; all I asked you to do was take out the trash!" Before I even walk out the door, I've spent ten dollars of my emotional energy as shown on the following ledger entry.

Description of Transaction	Deposit	Expenditure	Balance
			$50.00
Heated words with family		$10.00	$40.00

Then I get in the car and run into some traffic problems or have car trouble. This was unexpected, and it's putting some time pressures on me. My shoulders get tense, my teeth clench, I mutter a few complaints to myself, and the muscles in my body get tight. Without realizing it, I've spent five dollars of my emotional energy on that traffic or car problem.

Description of Transaction	Deposit	Expenditure	Balance
			$50.00
Heated words with family		$10.00	$40.00
Traffic problems		$5.00	$35.00

Then there's a problem waiting for me as I get to the office or classroom. Before I can get my coat off or get a cup of coffee, the telephone is ringing with an irate caller, or a student runs up and whines, or a coworker starts complaining, or my boss dumps another crisis on me. I'm thinking, "Can't they at least let me get my coat off?" And the blood pressure and stress levels rise. Here, again, I spend ten dollars of my emotional money.

Description of Transaction	Deposit	Expenditure	Balance
			$50.00
Heated words with family		$10.00	$40.00
Traffic problems		$5.00	$35.00
Irate caller		$10.00	$25.00

Midmorning the computer goes down, or some other needed equipment fails, and I'm at its mercy. My plans are delayed, inter-rupted. That bugs me! So I spend five dollars of my emotional money on the equipment problem, complaining with my cowork-ers about how nothing ever works around here.

Description of Transaction	Deposit	Expenditure	Balance
			$50.00
Heated words with family		$10.00	$40.00
Traffic problems		$5.00	$35.00
Irate caller		$10.00	$25.00
Equipment problem		$5.00	$20.00

Later on in the morning, my manager approaches me with another priority, another report, or another job that has to be done right away. My manager should know I've still got three crises left over from yesterday. I think, "If they could just get their act together around here and decide what they want me to do instead of dropping a new crisis on me every day...." Now this really bugs me, and I'm spending ten dollars of my emotional energy on it.

Description of Transaction	Deposit	Expenditure	Balance
			$50.00
Heated words with family		$10.00	$40.00
Traffic problems		$5.00	$35.00
Irate caller		$10.00	$25.00
Equipment problem		$5.00	$20.00
Work load crisis		$10.00	$10.00

An hour later a coworker—the one who has the annoying habit that gets under my skin—does whatever it is that bugs me, and I'm griping to myself about him or her and spending another ten dollars on that situation.

Wait a minute! It's only noon, and I'm emotionally broke. I've spent my whole fifty dollars on these little negative happenings, and for the rest of the day I'm living in overdrawn mode, running on fumes. That means stress takes over.

Description of Transaction	Deposit	Expenditure	Balance
			$50.00
Heated words with family		$10.00	$40.00
Traffic problems		$5.00	$35.00
Irate caller		$10.00	$25.00
Equipment problem		$5.00	$20.00
Work load crisis		$10.00	$10.00
Annoying coworker		$10.00	$0.00

When stress takes over, my attitude plummets immediately into minus territory, my body suffers, my performance suffers, my relationships suffer, my testimony for Jesus suffers. Why? Because when I'm in overdrawn mode, I say things I wouldn't normally say; I do things I wouldn't normally do; I overreact very easily; I get my feelings hurt at the drop of a pin; I focus on myself rather than on others; I go into self-pity, and anger gnaws at me.

Because I used up my emotional resources on things that weren't worth it and didn't spend my energy wisely, my attitude has suffered even before I realized it. It just happened, one little thing at a time. I didn't sit there thinking, "Wow, I'm getting a bad attitude." Or, "I'm going to be negative." No, I just allowed those little negative things that bugged me to use up all my energy and resources.

Now I start to get wise and decide that, as with my financial bank account, I have to watch how I spend my emotional money because there is not an unlimited supply. So I start talking to myself a lot:

"Mary, is it worth it?"

"Mary, what difference will this make in twenty-four hours?"

(Rule of thumb: If it doesn't make any difference in twenty-four hours, it's not worth any emotional energy.)

"Mary, is the world still revolving? Is God still in control? Has Jesus stopped loving you? Did the Lord forget you or forsake you?"

When I think this way, then I decide not to let something as unimportant as clothes on the bathroom floor or taking out the trash affect me, and I save that ten dollars.

Description of Transaction	Deposit	Expenditure	Balance
			$50.00
No heated words with family		$0.00	$50.00

Then I make a choice not to spend any money on the traffic problem, because after all, I have no control over that traffic and no amount of fretting is going to speed it up. (Note: If this happens often, I need to start leaving home earlier to avoid that stress factor.)

Description of Transaction	Deposit	Expenditure	Balance
			$50.00
No heated words with family		$0.00	$50.00
Traffic problems		$0.00	$50.00

When the irate caller or whining student approaches me, I remember, "Mary, this goes with the territory. It's part of your job, and it shouldn't surprise you to discover that you have to deal with this person. Don't take it personally." Notice that when you don't take something personally, you won't spend emotional money on it! Difficult people can't get to you when you don't allow them to lay guilt trips on you or cause you to get defensive and take it personally.

Description of Transaction	Deposit	Expenditure	Balance
			$50.00
No heated words with family		$0.00	$50.00
Traffic problems		$0.00	$50.00
Irate caller		$0.00	$50.00

So I don't spend that ten dollars on the irate person, and the same is true for the broken computer. Again, it's beyond my control, and getting upset doesn't make it work. So I save that five dollars. Keep in mind that through all of these things I'm talking to myself, getting my perspective back, and evaluating how I'm spending my emotional money.

Description of Transaction	Deposit	Expenditure	Balance
			$50.00
No heated words with family		$0.00	$50.00
Traffic problems		$0.00	$50.00
Irate caller		$0.00	$50.00
Equipment problem		$0.00	$50.00

Already I'm twenty-five dollars to the good because I've made choices at each of those situations to control my response, through the power of the Holy Spirit, and not let them control me. The work load priority problem really does bug me, but instead of ten dollars, I hold it to five dollars. And the coworker who gets to me I hold to five dollars.

Description of Transaction	Deposit	Expenditure	Balance
			$50.00
No heated words with family		$0.00	$50.00
Traffic problems		$0.00	$50.00
Irate caller		$0.00	$50.00
Equipment problem		$5.00	$45.00
Work load crisis		$5.00	$40.00

Instead of being broke at noon, I've got forty dollars left in my emotional account. I'm not running in stress mode; my attitude is still in positive territory. I'll handle things much better throughout the day. Why? Because I'm learning to pick my fights, to spend the emotional money when it makes sense but not let the little stuff wipe me out.

Now if that sounds crazy to you, I apologize, but quite frankly, it's a mental exercise I use almost daily to help me adjust my perspective on things. I tend to let little things wipe me out very easily, and this practice helps me to apply biblical truth.

Your enemy, Satan, does not want you to remember God's truth, so in the midst of a tough day, the principles you know you should practice just escape you, and you get to the end of the day and realize you lost because you forgot to practice what you know. This little exercise is my way of remembering and putting into practice the principle of changing the negatives to positives, coping with the little stuff, and keeping my thoughts within the boundaries of Philippians 4:8. Try it; you may find it helpful as well.

Watch Your Self-Talk

Check up on your self-talk. Many times we add a lot to our stress levels by the words we say to ourselves. Are you feeding too much negative junk back into your head on a daily basis? Things like: "I'll never get all this done," or "I know it's going to be a bad day," or "I'm so tired," or "I can't get along with him"? Please watch the negative self-talk. You can't control what other people say to you, but you can choose what you say to yourself. If you will avoid the wrong kind of self-talk, you will save yourself considerable stress.

Don't Be Intimidated
by Negative People

Do you work or live with someone who is a very negative person? Have you noticed that negative people tend to poison the atmosphere? That negative person can poison your mind if you don't protect yourself against the negative chatter. It seems to me that negative people are far more successful at making positive people negative than positive people are at making negative people positive. (Did you follow that?) I've never seen negative people embarrassed by their negative attitudes; they don't apologize for them. But they can make you feel like an idiot for trying to be positive.

Fight back. You don't have to apologize for being positive, nor should you feel embarrassed or intimidated. Keep telling yourself that while they have the right to be negative if they choose to, you have an equal right to be positive. Here are some ways to respond to those negative people:

- Tune out their negative talk. Hum a tune to yourself; think of something unrelated; barricade your mind against their negativity. Just don't listen.
- Don't spend any more time with really negative people than you

have to. If you have learned that they are going to be negative no matter what happens, then try to avoid having lunch or breaks with them or being around them at any time that it is not necessary. If you can find a way to work separately from them, without being offensive or obvious, then do so.

- Change the subject. When negative people start their negative talk, just change the subject to something neutral or positive. One person learned to respond to the negative chatter of her coworkers with a simple "Really?" Then she would proceed to change the subject. It can be a subtle, inoffensive way to get rid of the negative talk.
- Ask for a solution. When negative people start complaining about things, respond by asking, "Well, you've made some interesting points. Now, what is the solution to the problem? What would you do to change the situation?"
- Respond with positives. Reframe the negative statement. When they complain about the job, you can say, "Well, for sure everything's not perfect here, but at least we have a job. Lots of people would be real happy to have any kind of a job." Remember, you don't have to apologize for being positive. They may respond even more negatively, but don't be intimidated. Just stay on the positive high ground.

You just can't afford to let others fill your mind with their negativism because that poisons your mind and gives you a bad attitude.

Remember What Goes With Your Territory

There are certain negatives inherent in any job and in any situation. Even if you have a job that you love, there are things that go with that job that can destroy your attitude. For example, I have to travel a great deal in my business training profession. Believe me, travel is not glamorous. It involves late flights, lousy airline food, lost luggage, smelly hotel rooms, carrying heavy luggage, etc.

When I first began this job, I let every travel inconvenience bug me, and my attitude suffered greatly. Then it dawned on me (I'm a slow learner!) that travel simply goes with my territory, and if I can't handle it, then I have to get out of the business I'm in. But what I cannot do is allow the things that go with my profession to bring me down.

Some negatives inherent in your job may be:

- If you work with customers, you will sometimes have to deal with people who are irate, demanding, rude, unappreciative, or just plain dumb. That shouldn't surprise you—as long as you deal with customers that will always be the case. When you pick up the telephone, or face in person the frustrated, irate customer, you should think, "Oh, I expected this. I'm paid to deal with irate customers. It goes with my job." When you do that, you are in control, and you don't spend any emotional energy on the situation because you refuse to take it personally.
- If you deal with people's money, you can expect normally sane people to go into temporary insanity over a small money problem. That's the way money affects people, so it goes with your territory.
- If you are a government employee, people think you work for them and they pay your salary (which, incidentally, they do!). For this reason, you may have to deal with people who are demanding or pushy because they think you owe them something.
- If you are in a medical profession dealing with sick people or their family members, they are worried, fearful, upset, and ill. They won't behave as well in your environment as they would

under normal conditions and may need more sensitivity and understanding.

- If your business requires a great deal of travel, the travel inconveniences I mentioned earlier go with your territory.
- If your product or service is very expensive for your customers, the expense will cause a greater reaction and overreaction to any problem or complaint.

I conducted some customer service training in an insurance company where the employees were experiencing some unusual stress factors. Almost overnight the company had received a very large contract, which increased their work load significantly. Many new employees were brought on board to help, but the normal learning curve meant it would be several months before these new employees would be able to carry their load.

Meanwhile, the experienced employees were faced with an intensive work load along with an influx of new people who needed help and training. Also, their physical environment was under a great deal of change as desks and offices were shuffled and reshuffled to make room for the new employees. Everyone's work space was growing smaller and changing frequently.

Although the company was working feverishly to accommodate the growth, this success meant a temporarily difficult work situation. Several employees talked with me about this, with many complaints and gripes. They wanted these problems to go away and go away fast!

Finally I said to them, "You are living through the trauma of overnight success. While it brings some temporary inconveniences, it also means you have greater job security and more opportunity for advancement because your company is doing well. And this comes in an economy where many other companies are in a downsizing mode. These are negatives that go with your territory, and as I see it, you have three options in dealing with these negative aspects of your company's success."

The options I gave them were:

1. Keep griping and complaining about the negatives. That won't solve anything, and it will only add to your stress and bad attitude. But it is an option—unfortunately, one that many people choose.
2. Accept these temporary inconveniences with good grace, recognizing that they bring positives as well as negatives.
3. Quit and find another job. (Of course, it will have its own inherent negatives, which you will have to confront!)

Basically that's true for all of us when we're facing negatives that are inherent to our jobs. Remind yourself of what goes with your territory, and remember that you have a choice. It doesn't take a rocket scientist to figure out that choice number one is a lose-lose choice. Choice number three is the right choice in a few situations, but running away rarely solves anything. Choice number two is usually the best, and it is a win-win choice in dealing with the negatives inherent in your job.

Count Your Blessings

It's so easy for us to be focused on the negatives and forget all about the positives. Recently a good bit of my jewelry was stolen from a hotel room. Obviously that didn't make me happy, and I was doing everything possible to try to find it. The local police came to take my report, and the hotel security people were doing all they knew to help me. They kept apologizing to me, but I said to them, "Well, it's just jewelry. I haven't been notified that any of my family is sick or has a problem; I still have good health. This won't change my life in any significant way. I have so much to be thankful for that I refuse to let this unfortunate incident get to me."

Have you learned to stop and count your blessings in the middle of a bad day? It is such a good way to get your perspective back. We get thousands of letters every month from the listeners to my radio program, and many of them tell of very unfortunate and difficult situations. Any time I'm feeling sorry for myself, I start reading my mail, and I'm instantly reminded that I have it so much easier than many others. It causes me to count my blessings.

One person gave me a good idea. She keeps a folder of the positive things that have happened to her—the nice letters from managers or customers, awards she has received, affirmations or recognitions for work well done, copies of good appraisals, anything that documents the good things that have happened to her. Then when she starts to feel like she is worthless or a failure, or when lots of bad things happen to her in a day, she pulls out her folder and rereads those letters and good reports. That's a good way to practice Philippians 4:8—thinking about the good reports rather than the bad ones.

Look around you. You'll see many people in worse conditions than you are in. Reach out to help them, but be sure to count your blessings.

Your Day Is Won or Lost in the Morning Hours

How do your days normally begin? Rushed, hectic, fighting the clock? Are you grouchy in the morning, tending to have unkind words and arguments with those you live and work with? If you will make it a project to start your days better, your attitude will improve immensely because the day is won or lost in those morning hours!

Set the alarm earlier, and put the clock on the other side of the room so that you have to get up to turn it off. If you will discipline yourself to start your day earlier, in a relaxed fashion, with quiet time and a little leisure time at the beginning of the day, with kind words and patience toward your family and coworkers, you'll discover what an improvement you'll have in your attitude.

Use an Attitude Checkup Regularly

I want to encourage you to become much more aware of your attitude and determine to choose to be positive—to make better choices all day long every day. Remember, your attitude is always your choice. I'm including my own personal attitude checkup form for you to use if you wish to. Attitude can't be taught, but it can be learned if you will be your own teacher. The exercise on the following pages may help.

Attitude Checkup Form

Where does my attitude fall on this scale?

0	10	20	30	40	50	60	70	80	90	100
Totally Negative					Half and Half				Totally Positive	

- ☐ mostly positive (above 80 range)
- ☐ more positive than negative (60 to 80 range)
- ☐ half positive, half negative (40 to 60 range)
- ☐ more negative than positive (30 to 40 range)
- ☐ mostly negative (below 30 range)

What are the things or people that tend to ruin my positive attitude?

_____   _____

_____   _____

_____   _____

Plan of action:

1. I will pray about each of these negatives daily.
- pray for understanding and compassion
- pray for endurance
- pray for God's perspective

2. I will confront and try to change the following negatives:

_____   _____

_____   _____

_____   _____

3. I will learn to compensate for or reframe the following negatives:

_____   _____

_____   _____

4. I will accept the following negatives because they go with my territory:

_____   _____

_____   _____

5. I will avoid negative self-talk. Most of my negative self-talk happens at these times:

_____   _____

_____   _____

6. I will save my emotional energy for important issues rather than things that don't really matter. Often I overreact and spend too much emotional energy on:

_____   _____

_____   _____

_____   _____

7. I will not allow the negative people around me to poison my mind. These are the names of those negative people, and my plan for responding to them:

Negative People   My Response

_____   _____

_____   _____

_____   _____

Chapter Two

The Importance of First Impressions— and Second—and Third

I walked into the emergency room. I had been hired to conduct a long-term customer service training program for this large Chicago hospital. My first week's assignment was to familiarize myself anonymously with the hospital in order to gather information on where improvement was most needed to make the hospital more user-friendly.

The nurse behind the counter scowled at me. Well, she didn't actually scowl at me, because she never gave me any eye contact. She looked as if she had been eating lemons all day. Her face and body language were anything but friendly and inviting.

I thought, "I would never want her to be my nurse! I'd intimidated to even talk to her. Why would they put someone like that in such a high-profile job?"

Later I learned that this nurse had been with the hospital many years and was, according to her managers, one of the best they had. She really cared about her patients and did her job with excellence. But her management recognized that she made a very bad first impression and asked me to counsel with her one-on-one. As I did, I realized this was an unusual woman who had survived many adversities and was truly outstanding in her job. But she made a terrible first impression. Did she do it on purpose? Of course not! She had no idea people were perceiving her initially in a negative way. But the very negative first impression she gave to people was affecting her ability to really thrive on her job. It was holding her back, and it was totally unnecessary.

What Impression Do You Make?

Did you ever think about what kind of impression you make on people? I'm sure you've heard it said that first impressions are the most important, and you never get a second chance to make a first impression. That's true, but it's also true that last impressions are ones we remember, and all those in between are important too.

If you're not making consistently good impressions on your job, you're going to find it difficult to thrive. Making good impressions is not some phony, hypocritical facade we put on; it's not polishing the apple or playing company politics. It is simply being certain we're putting our best foot forward and making the effort to improve our skills and eliminate bad habits so that people remember the positive things about us rather than the negative ones.

Proverbs 14:8 says, "The wisdom of the prudent is to give thought to their ways." A prudent person is a wise, judicious, and careful person, and that person will give thought to his or her ways. Are you a prudent person? When was the last time you gave serious thought to your ways—your habits, your skills, the impression you make on others? I am certainly not advocating self-absorption but rather self-improvement—thinking about how your ways help or distract, encourage or tear down, make you look bad or good.

In the fifteenth verse of Proverbs 14 we read, "A simple man believes anything, but a prudent man gives thought to his steps." Are you willing to believe anything about yourself without checking it out, without facing the facts? Do you continually assume you're making a good impression instead of giving thought to how you're doing and how others interpret your actions and words?

As Christians working in a world that needs to know Christ, we should make the best impression we can. We are, after all, ambassadors for Jesus Christ; we represent him to our world.

Paul wrote, "For we are taking pains to do what is right, not only in the eyes of the Lord but also in the eyes of men" (2 Cor 8:21). *Taking pains to do what is right*—that's a good way to put it, because it really does take effort and concentration (and sometimes pain) to do what is right.

Perception Equals Reality

"Perception equals reality" is a good motto to keep in mind. We are all really good at judging books by their covers, quickly jumping to first impressions, and forming instant perceptions of people and situations. Whatever perception we form in our minds of others or they form of us, that becomes reality, whether or not it is true or correct.

Recently Steve, a participant in one of my business seminars, told me that he had a bad habit of putting his foot in his mouth and upsetting customers unintentionally. "I just seemed to be able to say everything the wrong way every time, and though I never intended to hurt feelings or cause problems, I was doing a good job of it." Therefore, the perception many customers had of Steve was negative, thinking him to be rude and inconsiderate, when in reality he wasn't at all that way.

Steve's boss suggested that he tape all of his conversations with his customers, and the boss would listen to those tapes later on to try to help him correct this problem. Steve said to me, "Mary, you wouldn't believe the change in me once I realized my conversations were being taped and my boss was going to listen to them. I started thinking about what I was saying, choosing my words much more carefully, and my foot-in-mouth problem went away practically overnight!"

Steve became aware that perception equals reality, got in touch with how he was perceived by others (with a little help from his manager), and raised his awareness level of his choice of words. Immediately he improved his image in the minds of his customers because he realized that perception equals reality.

The Consequences of Perception

Each of us must recognize that the consequences of perception are the same, whether or not the perception is accurate. You and I will suffer the consequences of how people perceive us, even though they may judge our book by its cover, jump to wrong conclusions, and perceive us in ways that do us a disservice.

Therefore, it behooves us to get serious about making certain that we do everything we can to make the best possible impression on people. If we are doing something that causes a negative reaction and it's something we can change, then we need to know what it is and be willing to change it.

Let me hasten to say that I realize you cannot please everyone. Somebody won't like the way you do it, no matter what. Nor can we ask perfection of ourselves, and we must learn to give ourselves room and time to grow and learn. We certainly don't want to live in a people-pleaser mode, where we are obsessed with trying to please other people. That is self-defeating and degrading.

However, the smart person is going to want to find out what kind of impression he or she makes and how it can be improved. It may be a painful lesson sometimes, but it's worth the pain. We have the most to gain by improving how others perceive us since we are the ones who suffer the consequences of how we are perceived.

Our Need for Perception Feedback

Few people go to work with the intention of doing a bad job. How many times have you said to yourself, "Now, what can I do today to really upset a few customers?" Or, "How can I make my manager really angry today?" Never! In fact, if I could sit down and talk to each of you, I'm sure you'd tell me how hard you work and how much you try to do things right. Most of us are trying to do a good job, and because we have good motivation, we can't imagine that others could perceive us differently.

If we don't have ways of getting perception feedback, however, we never really know where we need to improve, and we keep making the same mistakes over and over. That is simply because it is not easy to see and hear ourselves the way other people see and hear us.

Going Through React Mode

A problem often arises when we get some perception feedback that we didn't want or expect in the form of a criticism. Who likes criticism? Not me, especially when I think it's not fair or deserved.

I remember conducting a seminar at a church for a large group of women, and I thought things were going just fine. About midday, however, someone gave me a note—a very nicely written note, but a very direct criticism. Although the note was worded as nicely as possible, I have to tell you that my first reaction was not,

"Oh, thank you for sharing this with me." No, it was what I call *react mode*. I reacted, and my first thought was, "Who does she think she is, sending me this note?" Then I got defensive and thought, "Well, you ought to try to get up here and do this; it's not nearly as easy as it looks." Then self-pity set in, and I thought, "Who needs this? I didn't come all the way from Chicago to get criticized!"

I have a feeling you can relate to react mode. I used to think that I needed to learn to avoid react mode. Frankly, I've given up on avoiding it, because I think it's a normal human reaction to respond defensively to unpleasant words or criticism, even when they're given in a constructive way. My goal now is to get out of react mode as quickly as I can, and while I'm in it, to keep my mouth shut! If you talk in react mode, you'll say lots of things you'll wish you hadn't.

When my emotions calmed down a bit, I sat down and reread the note and thought about her advice. I realized she was giving me some very valuable perception feedback. I can assure you I had no intention of making a bad impression on that group of women. I thought I was doing a good job. Furthermore, I had never thought that what I said could be interpreted the way this note pointed out to me; it had simply never occurred to me.

I needed that perception feedback so that I could know how my audience perceived me. Otherwise I would keep on doing what I thought was right and making a less-than-favorable impression on my audience. I can never improve my skills and abilities without perception feedback. The more I can put myself in the shoes of my audience, the better I will be as a presenter and speaker.

How to Get Perception Feedback

If you really want to thrive, not just survive, on your job, you need to be open to perception feedback. Invite it and receive it because that's the only way you can know what you're doing or not doing that may be creating a less-than-favorable impression.

Steve, the man with the foot-in-mouth problem, had a positive response to his perception feedback, and he used it as an opportunity to improve. He could have chosen to stay in react mode, get defensive, blame the customers, get upset with his manager, and in the process raise his blood pressure and stress levels and damage his relationship with his manager. That would have been a lose-lose reaction. Instead he chose a win-win approach: He admitted his problem with saying things abruptly, and he was willing to take some specific action to correct it. He didn't stay in react mode; he moved on to solution stage.

Lots of people stay in react mode; they live there. They take everything personally and get their backs up easily, and they refuse to accept perception feedback. When you do that, you not only don't thrive on your job, you shrivel up. Promotions pass you by. Getting up and going to work each morning is a major drudgery. Your stress levels are high, and your performance deteriorates.

If you and I are ever going to grow and thrive in our jobs, we must not only accept but solicit perception feedback. Here are some suggestions to help you do that:

1. Start thinking on a regular basis, "How am I perceived by people who work with me, by customers, by managers? How do I come across to people who can't read my mind, who don't know what my intentions are, who perhaps have had no other experience with me?" The more you sensitize yourself to how

others perceive you, the more you'll be aware of what you do and say that is not making a good impression.

2. Ask for perception feedback. It's so much easier to accept criticism when you solicit it. When was the last time you asked your manager to give you some feedback on how you could improve your performance? And managers, when was the last time you asked your employees how you could better help them do their jobs?

3. Make a covenant with yourself and the Lord that you will not live in react mode and that you will make a conscious effort to keep your mouth shut while you're in react mode.

4. Accept criticism, even the criticism that is not given in the best way, as an opportunity for perception feedback. Try to filter out the emotional element and ask yourself if this criticism has validity. Force yourself to think more and more objectively about yourself.

5. Find ways to get more perception feedback. Record and listen to your voice. Record telephone conversations. Videotape your presentation and have others critique it for you. Take advantage of any training opportunity you can find to help you do a better job at getting more perception feedback.

6. Most importantly, pray for insight into how others perceive you. Ask God to show you your hidden errors (see Ps 19:12) and when he does, put them on your prayer list and pray specifically for help in those areas.

Whatever annoying habits or traits you now have that keep you from making a good impression, they will get worse as you get older. If you don't correct them now, they'll be much more difficult to correct next month or next year. What may be a little annoying at this stage in your life can drive people nuts in ten or twenty years! So, the sooner you get at it, the better.

Preparing for Perception Feedback

One other important principle we need to keep in mind as we tackle this challenge of improving the way others perceive us is that our spiritual health and maturity have a great deal to do with our ability to handle perception feedback. The more we are confident that our relationship with God is never based on performance, and appreciate how he has created and designed us, the easier it is for us to take an honest look at ourselves and admit our weaknesses.

If pursuing a knowledge of God is your highest priority, you're going to discover that facing the music as to where you need to improve and owning up to your need for change won't be nearly as painful and difficult as you think it will be. For every Christian, the issues of our lives, whatever they are, always come back to our relationship with the Lord. It is the building block that is necessary for all that we do, and it is the underpinning that carries us through the good and bad times.

When we find it very difficult to admit we're wrong, to accept criticism, to be open to suggestions for improvement, to truly desire to know how we are perceived, it may be a danger signal that tells us our relationship with God is not on sure footing. If that is the case, it is always *our* problem, not God's. He is waiting for us to draw near to him.

Prepare yourself for perception improvement and feedback by a review of your spiritual maturity and your pursuit of God.

Plan for Perception Improvement

To help you get started in improving the impression you make on others, candidly answer the following questions about yourself.

Check any of the following bad habits that you have:

- ☐ interrupt people often when they are talking
- ☐ chew gum frequently in public
- ☐ yawn often while others are talking to me
- ☐ finish other persons' sentences when they are talking
- ☐ jingle money in my pocket a lot
- ☐ tap a pencil on the desk or table during a conversation
- ☐ twist my hair while talking to others
- ☐ fail to give strong eye contact when talking to others
- ☐ have a weak handshake
- ☐ have a noticeable verbal crutch, such as *uh, you know, OK,* or *like*
- ☐ tend to use slang expressions or incorrect grammar often
- ☐ slouch when I'm sitting
- ☐ walk with poor posture or shuffle my feet
- ☐ have sloppy dress habits such as hanging shirttails or wrinkled clothes
- ☐ let my hair go ungroomed, uncombed, or dirty
- ☐ have dirty or unkempt fingernails
- ☐ tend to speak in an abrupt tone of voice
- ☐ answer questions in a condescending manner or tone
- ☐ talk too fast
- ☐ talk too loudly
- ☐ talk too quietly
- ☐ have bad breath due to improper hygiene or care
- ☐ eat with my mouth open

☐ gulp down food too fast
☐ talk with my mouth full of food
☐ slurp when I drink
☐ smile very seldom
☐ don't initiate greetings with others, such as "good morning"
☐ stare at people
☐ use finger-pointing phrases often, putting others on the defensive
☐ get defensive and take up for myself easily
☐ lose my temper often

If you have answered these questions honestly, your perception score is as follows:

Number of answers checked	You are creating
1-5	excellent perception
6-10	good perception
11-15	fair perception
16-20	poor perception
More than 20	very bad perception

Here are some ways to get better perception feedback:

1. Have a good and trusted friend give you his or her answers to these questions about you and see if your perception of yourself is markedly different from his or her perception of you. (In fact, you could do the same for your friend and help him or her with perception feedback.)

2. Make a plan for some perception feedback. Which of the following suggestions would you be willing to do in order to help you get feedback on how you are perceived by others?

☐ Solicit critiques and feedback from my manager or some other trusted person.

☐ Accept any criticism I receive as an opportunity to consider how I am perceived by others. Give it consideration, and if there is something constructive in the criticism, work on it and change.

☐ Put a plan in place to eliminate the bad habits I noted in question 1. (You do this through reminders, gimmicks, and accountability. See chapter 3.)

☐ Record telephone conversations with customers, coworkers, friends, etc., and listen to how I sound on the telephone. (All you need is a tape recorder and a plug you can buy at *Radio Shack* that hooks into the tape recorder and suctions onto the telephone handset. The laws vary among states concerning recording telephone calls. It may be appropriate for you to advise the other person on the phone that you are recording the call for training purposes.)

☐ Practice my presentations with a video camera, or use video in some other way to see how I look to others.

☐ Other: _____

_____

3. In order to turn your good intentions into action, set some specific goals with time frames and make yourself accountable to someone. Ask them to contact you occasionally to check on your progress.

Chapter Three

Change: What's So Hard About It?

Orva came to work for me after retiring. She wasn't ready to retire, so at seventy she worked part-time to help me promote my new radio program. After being in the radio business for thirty-five years, she knew how to do it, and she had connections. What a blessing to have Orva on my team. She had the energy and drive of a forty-year-old.

BUT—there was this thing called a computer! She had never used one before, and I had computerized our operation from the beginning. In order to work for me, she would have to learn to use a computer. Most people would have said, "I can't learn to use a computer; I'm too old," and never even tried. But not Orva.

"I'm not going to let some machine get the best of me," was her attitude. So she tackled that computer. Only later did I learn how frightened she was of it; she never let on. But little by little she learned how to use that computer. By rote, for the most part, but efficiently and effectively.

Orva was willing to take a risk, to stick her neck out, and to change the way she had done things all through her career. She didn't try to talk me out of using computers; she knew it was the way of the future. So she changed herself.

Change—it's just a word. But when you try to change, you discover it's more than just a word—it's a challenge. Few of us welcome change into our lives; most people go kicking and screaming into any kind of change. It's risky; it's unknown; it's uncomfortable; it's hard work. No wonder we run from it. But we can never improve or grow without changing. Thriving from nine to five is directly related to your willingness to change.

Why Is Change So Difficult?

As a business trainer, I was hired to try to get people to change. So I've had lots of opportunities to watch how people react to the need for a change in the way they do things. And I'm well aware of my own reluctance to change. Even though I talk about change all the time and try to motivate change in others, I still find it difficult to change the way I do things. Why?

1. *Change takes time.* It has been said that it takes twenty-one days to make a new habit and sixty-five days to get rid of an old one. That means change is rarely a matter of snapping your fingers and doing it. It takes time and commitment. You've got to be willing to hang in there until the change is completed.
2. *Change is uncomfortable.* It simply doesn't feel right. Anytime we try something new, there is an awkwardness and unfamiliarity that make us feel self-conscious and insecure. We step out of that safe territory where we've been so long, and we feel as though all eyes are on us, waiting for us to fail and laughing at our efforts.
3. *It's easy to forget.* Since change takes time, we have to remember to change, to do things differently than before. And we easily forget! Often it is simply a memory problem.
4. *Change appears threatening rather than enriching.* How easy it is to stay in that defensive react mode, denying the need to change rather than facing the music and embracing change.
5. *Change takes discipline.* Undisciplined people rarely make changes in their lives because they're too lazy or disorganized.

Be Willing to Face Yourself

Here's one final barrier to change. Change requires admitting you're wrong, and many people just refuse to humble themselves and say, "I need to change." It's that old serpent pride that gets into our minds and hearts, and we rebel against change because we refuse to admit we need to change.

The disciples asked Jesus, "Who is the greatest in the kingdom of heaven?" (Mt 18:1). Jesus called a little child to him and said, "I tell you the truth, unless you change and become like little children, you will never enter the kingdom of heaven. Therefore, whoever humbles himself like this child is the greatest in the kingdom of heaven" (Mt 18:3-4).

In order to be a child of God, we have to change; that's what Jesus said. We have to admit we can't get there the way we are and be willing to humble ourselves and change. When Jesus told those people they had to change and become like children, not too many of them were willing to do that.

Now, how about today in your life and in mine? Is some stupid pride keeping us from saying, "You know, that's an area where I really need to change. By God's grace, I'm going to change for the better"?

Remember that God's love for you is absolutely steadfast, and unlike humans, he does not give or take away his love based on your performance or your qualifications. It will not take God by surprise when you discover an area in your life that is less than what it should be. He knows it already, and even knowing all there is to know about you, his love and concern for you have not budged one inch.

Jesus is not waiting to beat you on the head for your failures or shortcomings. He only desires to help you face yourself so that you can be delivered from those bad habits and harmful practices. He always has your best interest at heart, so you can be absolutely honest and open with God without any fear of rejection or retribution. Therefore, face up to yourself as honestly as you can. That's essential for any significant change to occur.

How Do We Start the Change Process?

Why is it you haven't changed those things about yourself that you know need changing? You say, "I've tried, Mary, but I just can't do it!"

Good! That's exactly where you need to start. Recognize you can't do it on your own. All of us have stories to tell about trying so hard to change some bad habit, making a New Year's resolution to start a good habit, promising ourselves and God we're going to change, only to wake up a few days or weeks later and have to confess that it didn't last; it didn't work.

In order to change, we first have to realize we can't do it. Sounds like a contradiction, but it's the truth. Paul wrote to the Corinthians that it's only when we see how weak we are that we can be strong (see 2 Cor 12:10). So often I become discouraged with my inability to change, and I just say, "Lord, I want to change, but I can't. I think it's impossible for me, Lord." When I finally give up, I can see the smile on his face and hear him say, "I've been waiting for you to realize you'll never make it on your own."

Today's humanistic philosophy tells us we can do and be anything we want to. "I can do all things"—that's what the world system wants you to believe. But it's a lie. You cannot do all things on your own, but you can do everything through Christ who gives you the strength (Phil 4:13). You and I can do all that God has ordained us to do, all he has commanded us to do, all he requires us to do. There's a world of difference between those two philosophies. When you realize you are not self-sufficient and you go to Jesus daily for strength because you know how weak you are, then the miracles start to happen.

Maybe you need to begin the change process by admitting that you can't. No need pretending with the Lord anyway. Tell him what he already knows: You can't change. But ask him to change you through his strength.

Once you've done that, you're at the starting gate. The next step is to pray the change into your life. You know what you need to change; pray about it every day. Remind yourself that the change will be uncomfortable at first, and make a commitment to live through the discomfort.

Then be willing to put the discipline in place that change requires. Make yourself accountable to someone else for that twenty-one- or sixty-five-day transition period in order to help you stick to your new discipline. Find gimmicks and reminders to jog your memory on a daily basis so you don't forget to change.

Remember, however, that you can't do it without the power of the Holy Spirit in your life. If you approach changing with the idea that you can do this through will power and determination, you're most likely to fail. If you know there is a change that God wants you to make, then you know he will give you the power to do it. God never asks us to do something in our own strength, because he knows how feeble we are.

During that transition period, be prepared for lots of quick prayer meetings with the Lord, where you say, "Help, Lord. My commitment is wavering; my discipline is dying; my memory is failing. I must have your strength, Lord. I now claim it and the promise you've given me in Philippians 4:13 that I can do everything through Christ."

Like everything else in the Christian life, you change by faith. If you're willing to step out in faith and follow through with these suggestions, you're in for some neat surprises. Change isn't easy, but it is very rewarding and very necessary for anyone who aspires to be like Jesus—and for anyone who truly wants to thrive on his or her job, not just survive.

How to Effect Change in Yourself

Let's say that I work for a good company and I am a good employee. I work hard, I have a good attitude, I know my job well, and I'm generally cooperative and helpful. However, for some reason, I have a very abrupt voice. Always have had this abrupt voice—just the way I talk.

Now let's say that you are a customer of my company, and you call one day and as it happens, I answer the telephone. The first thing you hear is my abrupt voice. I say the right words, but you hear the tone more than the words. The tone says, "I'm in a rush; why did you call now? I didn't want to answer the phone." Now, mind you, I don't think that way, but I sound that way.

Because you don't know me, you may start to form a bad impression of me. (Perception equals reality, remember?) As the conversation continues, I answer your questions and give you the information you need, but I continue to do so with this abrupt voice. Even though I am able to help you, you still have a very bad impression of me because of my abrupt voice.

After we hang up, you think or say to yourself or to others, "Wow, what a rude person she was." Then, it's likely you will translate your opinion of me to my company. "Did you ever talk to ABC Company? Those people are so rude!" Or, let's say you're the assertive type, so you decide to complain about me. So you call my office, ask for my manager, and tell her that you talked with me and I was rude to you on the telephone.

My manager now confronts me with this problem. "Mary, a customer called to complain that you had treated her rudely."

"What?" I reply. "Are you kidding me? I've never been rude to a customer."

After a few back-and-forths like this, my manager suggests that the problem is my abrupt voice. She says I need to work at eliminating the abruptness in my voice. That doesn't sit right with me. After all, my intentions are perfectly good, and can I help it that I happen to talk with an abrupt voice? That's the way I am! (By the way, I've noticed that we often use that phrase—"That's the way I am"—to excuse bad behavior or let ourselves off the hook when we see a change that is needed.)

But my manager keeps explaining to me that even though she and I recognize that I am not intentionally rude, I am perceived as rude because of my abrupt voice. My manager insists that the only way to change that perception is to change my voice. There's that word again ... *change.*

"Well," I say to my manager, "I really don't know how to change my voice. This is the way I've always talked." She says that even though I've used this abrupt tone all my life, I can still change. And she gives me some suggestions and ideas to help me.

Now here's my challenge. I've got to get from this rut called *Abrupt,* which I've been in for years, to a new rut called *Friendly.* I'm willing to try to change. If I'm ever going to make it from *Abrupt* to *Friendly,* I will need three things:

1. *Commitment and discipline.* I've got to make up my mind that no matter how long it takes or how uncomfortable it feels, I'm

going to stick with it until my tone becomes friendly rather than abrupt.

2. *Reminders and gimmicks.* To help me get through the twenty-one- to sixty-five-day transition period, I will need to find some helpful tools and reminders to keep me on track.

3. *Accountability.* In this case, the accountability may be unavoidable because my boss is going to check up on me. Many times I will have to produce my own accountability and make myself accountable to others.

So I'm ready to tackle the job of changing my voice from abrupt to friendly. I'm committed and willing to work at it. My boss has suggested that the right gimmick is to smile when I pick up the telephone and keep smiling while I talk. I've made a sign to put near my telephone that says, "Keep smiling," and I know my boss is going to check up on me. With those three tools in place, here I go:

The telephone rings. I talk to myself, "Mary, remember to smile." I put a smile on my face and pick up the phone. (I've just taken one baby step outside of my *Abrupt* rut.) However, I feel very foolish with this silly smile on my face, and I think everyone is looking at me (which, of course, isn't true). So about as fast as I put the smile on, it comes off again.

I hang up the telephone and talk to myself again: "You didn't do so well. Hang in with the smile longer next time." As the day progresses, I get a little more comfortable with the smile. However, after about two hours everything gets really busy and I simply forget. I'm back in my *Abrupt* rut like I always was.

A few hours pass, and I remember that I've forgotten to

change! So I talk to myself and take some more baby steps out of that *Abrupt* rut. Little by little I begin to make progress over toward that *Friendly* rut where I want to be.

I will have to work at this every day, and I'm likely to go in and out of that *Abrupt* rut regularly, but less and less often as the days tick off. If I am truly committed, and if I have gimmicks and reminders, and if I am not a quitter, what I will discover is that after two or three weeks my voice is just sounding friendlier. It won't be long now before I'm in that *Friendly* rut most of the time—without even thinking about it. In fact, my voice will sound friendly even when I'm not consciously smiling because I've changed the sound I've been hearing in my head, which means that I now have a naturally pleasant voice. The process is summarized in the following illustration:

Change: What's So Hard About It?

Abrupt   Friendly

Lasting change demands:
Time (21–65 days)

Commitment   Reminders

Gimmicks   Accountability

That's what change is like, and you can apply that scenario to any change you're trying to make in your life or your skills. For example, maybe you're committed to having a firmer handshake because you realize that wimpy ones give a very bad impression. You'll have to work at being comfortable with a firm handshake, not forgetting to have a firm handshake, and living through the transition period. Otherwise, you'll just continue to have the handshake that leaves people cold and gives a bad impression of you.

Use Early-Morning Rituals to Effect Change

Perhaps you could establish a little ritual at the beginning of each day that reminds you to change. Early-morning reminders are the best, before the day gets away from you. I practice several in my quiet time each morning and have been doing them for years. One of my daily routines is to dress the inner person, just as I dress the outer person. I remember to put on kindness and gentleness, peace and tolerance, thankfulness and patience before I leave home. That helps me remember to change in areas where I'm aware that I need to improve.

Use the following chart to record the changes you need to make and the steps you can take to accomplish them.

A Chart for Change

Using the three necessary steps to change, chart the changes you see needed in your own life.

Needed Changes (areas you know need some improvement)	Possible Gimmicks (techniques and reminders you can use to help you change)	Time Goal (21–65 days from your start date)	Accountability (a person who knows of your plan and will encourage you)
_____	_____	_____	_____
_____	_____	_____	_____
_____	_____	_____	_____
_____	_____	_____	_____
_____	_____	_____	_____
_____	_____	_____	_____
_____	_____	_____	_____
_____	_____	_____	_____
_____	_____	_____	_____
_____	_____	_____	_____

Chapter Four

Communication: The Name of the Game

The president of a midsize company was fed up with the cost of miscommunication within his company. "We're wasting time and money because we don't know how to communicate," he told his management team. "Beginning immediately we're starting a campaign called 'Say It Back to Me.' I want big banners made and posted all over the company. I want a memo sent to every person explaining this new campaign. I'm determined to improve our communication."

Over the next few weeks, employees began to get used to their president's new idea. In any business conversation, whether it was one-on-one, in a group meeting, or on the telephone, each employee had to conclude his statements with, "Will you please say it back to me?" The other person had to paraphrase what he or she heard that person say.

Of course no one liked it at first. It was a change, and as we've already seen, we don't take to change easily. But since it was the president's campaign, they realized they had little choice. So day by day everyone got more comfortable with "Say It Back to Me," which was a simple technique to make everyone aware of the importance of communicating clearly and unambiguously.

Twelve months later the company was able to identify a significant bottom-line, hard-dollars savings to the company because of improved communication. The reduction in errors and mistakes, plus the increased productivity because of saving the time required to fix those mistakes, was easily identifiable as a result of this simple campaign to improve communication. "But," the president said, "we received another benefit I hadn't counted on. This improvement in communication eliminated many bad feelings between employees and greatly increased our team spirit and *esprit de corps.* That has proven to be one of the best results of our campaign to communicate more effectively."

How many times have you said, "Wow, I didn't communicate with that person very well"? Or, "We really miscommunicated, didn't we?" I think communicating accurately and effectively is one of the best skills we can acquire and one of the toughest too. It simply is not easy to communicate, and in order to do it well, we have to learn the skills and work hard at improving and maintaining them in our own lives. Thrivers are good communicators and people who work at improving all the time.

Remember 2 Corinthians 8:21: "For we are taking pains to do what is right, not only in the eyes of the Lord but also in the eyes of men." Developing good communication skills requires some "pains," but it is effort that pays off in enhanced performance, improved relationships, and reduced stress.

How We Communicate: Verbally, Vocally, and Nonverbally

If we want to be better communicators, we need to understand the dynamics of this communication process. Generally we have three ways to send messages back and forth to each other:

1. Verbal communication—your choice of words
2. Vocal communication—the tone of your voice
3. Nonverbal communication—your body language, facial expressions, manner of dress, eye contact, posture, etc.

When I am in front of a group making a presentation, I am aware that they will hear more than just the words I say to them. If words were the only or even the most powerful way to communicate, we could all read everything and there would be no reason to verbalize those words. But my words will have more or less impact on that group depending on how well chosen they are, the enthusiasm of my voice, how I dress, and a number of other nonverbal techniques that will make a strong impression on my audience.

Interestingly, these means of communication vary in their impact. In other words, some are louder than others, as shown in the following chart.

As this chart shows, nonverbal communication is the loudest. What we see with our eyes has a stronger impression on us than what we hear, and the tone of voice is louder than the words we say. If you think about it, you realize that when you first meet someone, you usually jump to strong first conclusions based on what you see. Before that person opens his or her mouth, you have sized him or her up, often developing a strong impression.

(Pie chart: 55% nonverbal, 38% vocal, 7% verbal)

Once the person speaks, your impression is further developed by his or her voice. No matter how nice the words may be, if they are spoken with an abrupt tone or with a lifeless voice, the nice words will not sound nice. People hear the tone before they hear the words.

In the three chapters that follow, we will take an in-depth look at each of these three means of communicating. They are important enough in themselves to warrant significant discussion.

Developing Good Listening Habits

No discussion of communication would be complete without talking about listening skills. Are you a good listener? The quiz at the end of this chapter will help you answer that question.

Listening is a critical skill if you and I want to truly thrive on our jobs. Think what good listening will do for you:

- Good listening gives you more information, and information is power. We never learn anything while we're talking; listening gives us an opportunity to learn something. The more information you have in any situation, the more power you have because you're dealing from strength and knowledge, not weakness and ignorance.
- Good listening helps keep you out of trouble. When you listen better and longer, you're less likely to put your foot in your mouth and embarrass yourself. You just won't make a fool of yourself quite as often when you develop your listening skills.
- Good listening makes the other person feel important. That person will then like you better simply because you listened to him or her. So it improves relationships. I'm sure you can think of relationships you have where you often say or think, "He (or she) never listens to me!"
- Good listening helps you focus on other people rather than yourself. Anyone who is others-focused is much happier and more content than someone who is self-focused.

Identify Your Bad Listening Habits

There have been books and lectures given on listening, so this is a topic which could consume the whole book. However, I believe we can really improve our listening skills by a simple approach: Identify your worst listening habits and set goals to change them.

A few years ago I faced the reality that I am not by nature or personality a good listener. Some personality types simply listen better than others; they're born that way to some degree. However, a driver type like me does not usually inherit good listening skills. And I knew I needed to improve.

So I identified my worst listening habits and began a program to improve. I'm absolutely certain that I'm a much better listener today than three or four years ago. I also know I haven't arrived, and there's a long way to go. But the awareness of my rough edges really helped me change.

Consider this list of typical bad listening habits and ways to improve:

1. *Thinking of what you're going to say while the other person is talking.* Often we are simply waiting for our turn to talk instead of listening. We have something we're anxious to say, so we're formulating our next speech in our heads when we should be listening. This is a common bad habit for driver-type personalities and people in sales jobs, where we think our words are so important. The facts are, more sales are closed with good listening skills than with good verbal skills!

   Cure: Talk to yourself and remind yourself to listen. This can only be cured by increased concentration. In some situations it will help to take notes while listening. Where that is not possible, develop the mental ability to concentrate. If you want to, you can.

2. *Interrupting the other person.* This is an obvious bad habit that will irritate people greatly. Often we tend to interrupt others when we think they're wrong or when we get tired of waiting for them to finish.

   Cure: Tell people close to you not to let you get by with this bad habit. Give them your permission to stop you when you start to interrupt them. If they will do that for you, in a few days you'll be fed up with hearing "Excuse me, you interrupted me again," and you'll start changing that bad habit.

3. *Completing the other person's sentences.* Similar to interrupting, this bad habit will also interfere with good communication and irritate as well. This was and still is one of my strongest tendencies because of my intense focus on not wasting time. If people are having difficulty getting their words out, I get antsy and start talking for them. If you think about it, it's not only irritating, but also a bit arrogant and disrespectful to think you can talk for other people.

   Cure: Same as for interrupting.

4. *Mind wandering.* Distractions—both mental and environmental—can cause our minds to just take off in another direction and keep us from listening to what is being said. I often say that I can nod my head, have a sincere look on my face, and look you in the eye but not hear a word you've said because of my bad habit of mind wandering.

   Cure: Take notes while you're listening and eliminate distractions. When I started working on my mind-wandering bad habit, I made myself take notes whenever I could. On the telephone, in my office, at church, in a meeting—take notes of what the other person is saying. It forces you to concentrate and keep your mind from wandering. Those notes can come in very handy later on too.

Eliminate distractions that cause your mind to wander when you should be listening. I often try to do two things at once—listen and keep working at the computer, reading something else, or shuffling papers. But rarely are we truly capable of listening well while doing something else. Taking notes while I listen cures this problem as well.

You may need to work on environmental distractions: Noise around you, conversations of other people near you, loud music—these are some typical things we encounter in most job situations, and they can keep us from listening well. Use hand signals to ask others to move away from you while you're on the telephone. Think of what could be done to cut down on the noise level around you.

5. *Selective listening.* This is the bad habit of hearing part *a*, then tuning out for part *b*. You might tune out because you assume, after hearing part *a*, that you know what part *b* will be. Or maybe because you didn't like part *a*, you don't want to listen to part *b*. Actually it could work the other way around too: You did like part *a* and didn't want to hear any more.

    Cure: Raise your awareness level by putting signs around you that say, "Don't listen selectively." Remind yourself early in the day and all day long. Talk to yourself about listening all the way through, not just to part *a*.

6. *Biased listening.* When you carry a personal prejudice into a conversation, you are likely to be guilty of biased listening. For example, if you go to an auto-repair shop to get some advice on needed repairs to your car, you may be prejudiced if a woman

mechanic tries to help you. "What can a woman know about repairing cars?" you think. Even if she is an expert, you tend to tune her out because of a gender prejudice.

A woman I know used to teach English grammar, and she carried a bias toward anyone who used poor grammar. Once she heard or read something that was not grammatically correct, she dismissed that person as being uneducated and therefore not worthy to listen to.

Other biases would include generation or age bias, cultural bias, racial bias, or geographical bias. I noticed when I first moved to the North from Georgia many years ago with my then strong Southern accent, many people would repeat things to me as though I were hard of hearing. Gradually I realized it was a bias toward Southerners—a tendency to think that because of our slow speech patterns, we are a little slow mentally. That is an example of a geographical bias.

Cure: Identify your biases. Become more aware of your tendency to discount someone based on how he or she looks or dresses or his or her position, sex, or race—or whatever. The more you are aware of your biases, the more likely you will be to avoid them.

7. *Defensive listening.* This is the tendency to take everything personally and respond in a defensive mode. It can be an indication of a self-focused person, when someone thinks that everything is referring to him or her, or of a very insecure person, if he or she feels guilty so easily.

Cure: Remember that when you become defensive, you are headed for a problem of some type. It could be a fight with the other person, or getting your feelings hurt easily, or causing the other person to get defensive.

If any of these bad listening habits ring a bell with you, choose the one that is most obvious, and work on it. Remember our illustration about change. You won't break these bad habits overnight, but with commitment, gimmicks, reminders, and accountability, you can definitely see strong improvement.

Ways to Avoid Miscommunications

Often the problems we are trying to solve today began with some simple miscommunication yesterday, last week, or last month. It could be something as simple as a date or time that was misunderstood that ends up causing a lot of unnecessary stress.

Any effort to avoid miscommunication up-front pays off handsomely later on. These four suggestions can be used to clear up misunderstandings before they begin.

Be Aware of Communication Screens

Between every sender and receiver in any type of communication there are barriers that a communicator must hurdle in order to be understood clearly. I call them *screens* through which your communication must pass. This illustration shows some of the screens we deal with.

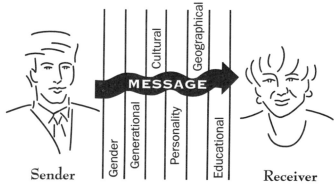

This is not an exhaustive list of the screens we encounter, but it gives some of the more common ones. Any screen may cause the message to be misunderstood in some way simply because we hear and understand differently based on our own backgrounds, experiences, education, etc. Therefore, if I want to eliminate miscommunication and misunderstanding, I have to learn to get my messages through the screens of the person I'm trying to communicate with.

For example, if I'm a woman talking with a man, I know there is a gender screen between us. I also know that men tend to communicate much more literally than women and aren't particularly good at reading between the lines. So even if I don't know the man I'm talking with really well, I can assume there is some likelihood of miscommunication if I'm not careful to maneuver through that gender screen and make certain my words are precise.

If I'm talking to a person who has an analytical personality, I know that person will require more details and ask more questions because of his or her personality. If I'm not willing to give that detail, it could cause a miscommunication.

If you want to thrive on your job, start becoming aware of the screens that exist between you and those you communicate with. Adjust for the screens to avoid miscommunication and misunderstanding. It makes life much simpler.

Repetition

Simply repeating what we've said or heard is probably the easiest way to solve most miscommunication problems. It begins with an understanding that we must not assume that we have communicated clearly but rather that there is a strong possibility we have *not* communicated clearly.

Always repeat numbers, dates, times, meeting places, etc. This is especially true when communicating by telephone, as the telephone lines seem to garble those numbers and instructions easily. In many cases it is smart to confirm these types of communication in writing. Any time you set an appointment, repeat it. Any time you agree to a schedule or time frame, repeat it. Any time you quote a price, repeat it. The few seconds of effort expended upfront can save you hours of headaches later on.

Paraphrasing

This is the say-it-back-to-me idea I described at the beginning of this chapter. A paraphrase usually begins with "Let me be sure I understand ..." or "So what you're telling me is ..." By using paraphrasing more often, you will clear up misunderstandings before they have a chance to grow. It also shows respect and caring and makes the other person feel special because you have taken the time to make certain you have heard him or her correctly.

Follow-Up

Telephone calls, faxes, memos, and letters are all good ways to follow up on any communication to make certain there is no misunderstanding. I find we have to do that often in my organization to eliminate frustrating and embarrassing miscommunications. We have established several systems of follow-up to go the extra mile in eliminating mistakes. We use forms we have designed, and we have standardized ways of handling certain information so that things don't fall between the cracks. And we continually look for ways to improve those systems.

Think of where you often are having to correct a mistake, explain a situation, or pick up after someone else's miscommunication. What could you do in advance to foresee those problems and keep them from occurring? It may not be in your job description, but it certainly will make your job easier.

Listener's Quiz

Check whether you usually, sometimes, or seldom do the following things when taking part in a conversation with an individual or group.

1. Respond to the speaker by a nod and brief confirming comments such as "Yes" and "I see"?
   ☐ usually   ☒ sometimes   ☐ seldom

2. Decide from the speaker's appearance and delivery whether or not what he or she has to say is worthwhile.
   ☐ usually   ☐ sometimes   ☐ seldom

3. Determine my own bias, if any, and try to allow for it.
   ☐ usually   ☐ sometimes   ☐ seldom

4. Keep my mind on what the speaker is essentially saying, repeating key words to myself where this will aid my memory.
   ☐ usually   ☐ sometimes   ☐ seldom

5. Interrupt immediately when I hear a statement that I feel is wrong.
   ☐ usually   ☐ sometimes   ☐ seldom

6. Make sure before answering that I've clearly understood the other person's point of view.
   ☐ usually   ☒ sometimes   ☐ seldom

7. Try to have the last word.
   ☐ usually   ☐ sometimes   ☐ seldom

8. Selectively listen, filtering out those messages that are not of importance to me.

☐ usually ☐ sometimes ☐ seldom

9. Listen defensively, taking everything personally.

☐ usually ☐ sometimes ☐ seldom

10. Frequently interrupt the speaker before he or she is finished.

☐ usually ☐ sometimes ☐ seldom

11. Think of what I'm going to say next as soon as the speaker comes up for breath.

☐ usually ☐ sometimes ☐ seldom

12. Mentally or verbally complete his or her sentences.

☐ usually ☐ sometimes ☐ seldom

How to Score Yourself

Questions 1, 3, 4, and 6:
For every "Usually" answer, give yourself 10 points.
For every "Sometimes" answer, give yourself 5 Points.

Questions 2, 5, 7–12:
For every "Sometimes" answer, give yourself 5 points.
For every "Seldom" answer, give yourself 10 points.

Total Points:

Below 60   You have developed some bad listening habits.
70–85   You listen well but could improve.
100 or above   You're an excellent listener.

Chapter Five

Improving Your Verbal Skills

I settled into my assigned seat on the airplane—a bulkhead seat, which meant I had no seat in front of me. The flight attendant advised me to put my attaché underneath my seat, which I did. Just as I was buckling up and getting ready for takeoff, a man took the seat behind me. Seeing my attaché, he stood over me, hands on hips, and said in a loud voice, "Move your attaché. It doesn't belong there, and I don't want it there. Move it right now!"

I moved my attaché. Actually I wanted to hit him with it, but somehow I resisted. For the remainder of that flight, however, I sat there with smoke coming out of my ears because of the way this passenger had spoken to me. Fifteen minutes later I was able to think of some wonderful retorts for him, but I had no opportunity to use them. (I can always think of good lines fifteen minutes late!)

The man's choice of words had made me angry. I didn't mind moving my attaché. All he needed to say was, "Would you mind moving your attaché so I can have more foot room?" I would have done so gladly and never given it a second thought. So, it wasn't the message—"move your attaché"—that bugged me. It was the choice of words.

This kind of scene happens on a regular basis in each of our lives, and particularly in our working worlds. We throw messages around carelessly without thinking about the impact those words will have on the other person and, all too often, without caring about the impact.

Using Words Like Bullets

People who are just surviving, not thriving, often use words like bullets. They have this kind of attitude: "I just say what I think; whatever is on my mind, that's the way I say it. If you don't like it, that's your problem, but I say what I think!" They even seem to be proud of this attitude, as though it is to be admired.

In reality what they are saying is, "I'm going to shoot off my mouth in any direction I choose, and if you get hit by the bullets, too bad." Not only do those people wound many others with their words, but they also shoot themselves in the foot by using words like bullets.

Proverbs 16:21 (NASB) says, "The wise in heart will be called discerning, and sweetness of speech increases persuasiveness." Sweetness of speech means sugarcoating words so they're easier to swallow. Anytime we do that, not only is it nice for other people, but we're far more successful in getting them to do what we want them to do. It's a win-win situation. On the other hand, using words like bullets is simply not smart, and it shows a real lack of understanding of the power of words.

The Bible says, "The tongue has the power of life and death, and those who love it will eat its fruit" (Prv 18:21). When you and I love to talk, we have to be prepared to eat the fruit of our tongues. Have you ever had to eat your words? They don't usually taste too good, do they? However, the more we are careful to choose words of life, not death, the sweeter our words will be to eat, both for us and those who hear our words.

You've probably heard the saying, "Sticks and stones may break my bones, but words will never hurt me." While there is some good advice in that slogan, we need to be aware that words can and do hurt very much. We've all been hurt by words, and some people have been hurt so deeply that they have difficulty recovering from the wounds those words caused.

How to Improve Your Verbal Skills

Thriving on our jobs will require close attention to our choice of words. Proverbs 21:23 says, "He who guards his mouth and his tongue keeps himself from calamity." In other words, we save ourselves large amounts of trouble and grief as we get better at choosing words that go down easy, not words that cause others to be upset, defensive, or negative. How do we improve our verbal skills?

How often I've wished there was a pill you could take to cure foot-in-mouth disease. Believe me, I am typically fast on the trigger with my words, and many times I have cringed to hear the words I just said. The problem is compounded because you can't *un*say those words. You can apologize and try to smooth things over, but once said, those words hang there between you, having done some damage.

So the smart thing to do is to hear your words before they come out. Raise the awareness level of your choice of words, constantly reminding yourself to hear what you're going to say. David wrote, "Set a guard over my mouth, O Lord; keep watch over the door of my lips" (Ps 141:3). I have written that verse in my prayer journal along with several others about the tongue and words, and I pray them into my life regularly. It has made a difference; my sensitivity to my choice of words is much greater than it used to be. While I have a long way to go, I am improving in my ability to hear those words before they are said, which can save a lot of grief later on.

Now when I say the wrong words, I usually am aware of it right away, and the taste of those bitter words in my mouth is a strong incentive to avoid saying them again. I learn a great deal by cleaning shoe polish off my face (from putting my feet in my mouth) and saying, "I'm sorry; I shouldn't have said that." That's one way to improve your verbal skills—painful, but effective.

Another way to improve verbal skills is to listen to others around you. You know, we can learn from both good and bad role models. Someone gave me some good advice early in my career. He said, "You can learn as much from a bad manager as you can from a good one." So learn by observing and listening to people around you. When you find someone who handles words really well, listen and analyze his or her choice of words. When you find someone who uses words like bullets, learn from their poor choice of words.

Avoiding the Wrong Words

When I was in sales training with IBM, I went through some exhaustive exercises to learn to say the right words to my prospects and customers. Knowing that sales opportunities are fragile, it was very important for me, as a sales representative, to be prepared with the right words when I finally had an opportunity to make my sales pitch.

Similarly, we need to be aware of verbal danger zones—times when the choice of our words becomes even more critical. We need to prepare ahead of time for these danger zones so that we choose our words carefully and appropriately.

Certain types of words we should avoid altogether. These include defensive words, I-don't-care words, bad-news words, dictatorial words, finger-pointing words, condescending words, careless words, and verbal crutches, bad grammar, slang, and buzzwords.

Defensive Words

Defensive words are so easy to say, especially when someone is pointing a finger at you. Everything in us wants to defend ourselves or our company or our friend when we feel we are being unfairly accused or blamed. But as soon as you use defensive words, you have set yourself up for failure.

Keep in mind that you want to be a problem-solving person, not a problem-escalating person. Defensive words escalate a problem, so avoid them. Bite your tongue if you have to, but don't allow yourself to use defensive words.

Try to avoid the whole issue of who's right and who's wrong, who did it and who didn't, and head straight for the solution stage. You are a problem-solver, so find words that will get you quickly to the problem-solution stage.

Instead of "It's not my fault," or "I didn't make that mistake," or "We didn't do that," say: "Well, it appears there has been some misunderstanding about this. But the important thing is to solve the problem. Let's see what we can do." Or, "I'm sorry there's been a misunderstanding. Let me see if I can help you."

With some version of that simple phrase—"there's been a misunderstanding"—you politely let the other person know you are not interested in proving who's right and wrong, but in solving the problem. That phrase sets you up for the solution stage and bypasses that time-consuming, unprofitable discussion about where to lay the blame.

Sometimes, to avoid defensive words, you can assume some responsibility even if you are fairly certain you've done nothing wrong. For example, if persons start in on the "You told me ..." line, instead of arguing with them that you did not tell them, say, "Well, I don't remember saying that, but my memory is pretty bad these days. At any rate, here's what we can do ..." or, "Perhaps I didn't explain that very well. Let me try again."

A thriver is not going to waste time or energy on useless defensiveness. The more you avoid it, the less stress you will have, the more effective you will be, and the more professional you will appear.

I-Don't-Care Words

How many times have you heard, "It's not my job," "It's not our department," or "I don't know"? I'm sure, like me, you've heard these more than you care to remember. When someone uses these words, it always sounds like that person doesn't care and is just trying to get rid of you.

Some better ways to give these messages include:

"I don't want to give you the wrong information. Perhaps Jim can help you ..."

"I'd be glad to help you with that if I could, but we don't have that information here."

"I'm probably not the most qualified person to answer that question. Let me put you in touch with ..."

"I don't know, but I'll find out."

"That's a good question. Let me put you in touch with someone who has a good answer."

Bad-News Words

How often are you required to tell someone something you know he or she doesn't want to hear? For example, "Your order has been delayed," or "He's not available," or "I can't get to that today." You know before you say it that it is bad news. The other person is not going to be happy about it no matter how nicely you phrase the message.

Any time you have bad news, the basic rule is: Soften the blow. Try to deliver the bad news in as easy a way as possible. Find a positive way to say a negative. Don't dwell on what you cannot do; get past that as quickly as possible to what you can do.

Instead of:

"We can't ship that order to you because your account is past due and our policy is ninety days."

Say:

"I certainly do want to release this order for you, and we can do that as soon as you can send us some payment on your account. There is an amount over ninety days past due, and if we could have even a partial payment, we would be able to ship this order right out to you. Could you overnight a check to us?"

Instead of:

"There's no way I can get that report finished today."

Say:

"If there were any way I could get it done for you today, I surely would. However, I believe I can probably get to it first thing tomorrow. How's that?"

When you can't do what someone has asked you to do, I find it helps to say "I wish I could" before you say "I can't." Then get to what you *can* do rather than focusing on why you can't. In that last example, I think it would be a mistake to say:

"You see, I've got five other reports due today, and there is an unscheduled meeting this afternoon that I have to attend. Besides, it's the end of the month, and Ms. Jones is expecting those month-end figures today. After all, I'm just one person."

Most of the time the other person doesn't want to hear why we can't do what we can't do. It can sound defensive and whiny pretty quickly. So just go to what you *can* do as quickly as possible.

Dictatorial Words

None of us likes to be told what to do. We naturally react poorly to dictatorial words. Try your best to avoid sounding like a dictator. Put your instructions in the form of a question; it works beautifully.

Instead of:
"You'll have to call back later."
Say:
"Could I ask you to call back later?"

Instead of:
"Have a seat; I'll be right with you."
Say:
"Would you please have a seat?"

Instead of:
"Hold on."
Say:
"Could I ask you to hold for a moment?"

Instead of:
"Fill out these forms."
Say:
"Would you mind filling out these forms?"

Instead of:
"Have this ready by two o'clock."
Say:
"Can you have this ready by two o'clock?"

If we could just learn this one little technique of asking rather than telling, we'd improve our verbal skills immensely. Start becoming more aware of how you give orders to people. Even when you have the authority to tell someone what to do, it's so much more motivating to ask than to tell. Make your job easier by choosing words that motivate rather than demotivate the other person.

Of course there are times when instructions must be given in a firm and decisive way. Obviously there are exceptions to every rule. But most of the time we will catch many more flies with honey than with vinegar, so ask, don't tell.

Finger-Pointing Words

How do you react when someone says to you, "You made a mistake," "Your figures are incorrect," or "You misspelled that word"? Finger-pointing words lead us into defensive words. So we want to be certain that we don't cause others to get defensive just because of our choice of words. (They may get defensive for other reasons, but at least we don't want to instigate it.)

When it is necessary to point out an error or mistake, use the face-saving method:

"I haven't checked the dictionary, but I think this word is spelled like this. Would you check it please?"

"Math is not my best subject, but it appears that column doesn't balance. Am I wrong?"

"I can see how you would come up with that answer, but have you also considered ...?"

Richard, a participant in my seminar on customer service, worked for a software company. His job was to help customers solve their software problems. Customers often called with what they were certain was a software problem, but it usually turned out to be a mistake they were making on the computer. Richard said, "I point out their mistake and solve their problem, but they still are upset with me for telling them it's their error, not the software."

I said, "You've been bruising their computer egos. Find a face-saver that doesn't point fingers at your customers." I suggested something like, "You know, many other customers have had similar problems; you're not the first one." Or, "I had a problem with that myself at first." Or, "It may be that our manual is not as clear on that point as it could be." Face-savers often keep the other person from getting defensive.

Condescending Words

"That's not a good idea." "That's so stupid." "That's a dumb suggestion." "Well, all you have to do is send in the form." "If you'd read the instructions, you'd see it's right there, easy as one-two-three."

Condescending words sound like the teacher talking to the student or the parent talking to the child—none of us adults like them. Watch out for those words that seem to say, "Stupid, why did you ask that dumb question?" Many times it's our choice of words coupled with the tone of our voices that gives a very condescending feeling.

I think it's particularly important to check our words when we're dealing with elderly persons or people who don't speak English as well as we do. In trying to communicate with them you can sound very condescending, treating them like children. Also, when talking to someone who has asked a question we consider unnecessary or dumb or to which the answer is obvious, we must be very careful about our words. It's easy to come across as condescending.

Careless Words

I could fill this book and a few others with examples of my careless words. Often they are words intended to encourage or to be funny, but they come out wrong.

My good friend Cynthia is studying to take her CPA exam for the second time. Just last Sunday I said to her, "We're going to pray you through this exam again." I was trying to be encouraging, but what it sounded like was, "You couldn't pass the test the first time, but we'll stick with you even though you're having to take it twice." (By the way, very few people pass the CPA exam the first time.) Thankfully, Cynthia is my good friend, and she laughed and immediately forgave me. But I wished I had said it differently. I regretted my careless words.

Not too long ago, in front of a group, I teased another friend when she mentioned her book. "That's a sneaky way to publicize your new book," I said, intending to sound funny. But instead it hurt her feelings, and I can understand why. I used careless words. Words that didn't need to be said. Words for which I apologized, but which can never be unsaid.

Proverbs 10:19 reminds us, "When words are many, sin is not absent, but he who holds his tongue is wise." I've noticed that when I say too much and just keep babbling on, pretty soon I'll say something I wish I hadn't. James put it this way: "Everyone should be quick to listen, slow to speak and slow to become angry" (Jas 1:19).

Jesus warned us, "But I tell you that men will have to give account on the day of judgment for every careless word they have spoken. For by your words you will be acquitted, and by your words you will be condemned" (Mt 12:36-37).

Verbal Crutches, Bad Grammar, Slang, and Buzzwords

We need to check out our verbal skills for these villains that can make us sound less professional, less articulate, or less educated, or can cause us to talk over the heads of our listeners.

Verbal crutches are words or phrases that are repeated so often that people start to count! Some of the more typical ones are:

you know	you know what I mean
OK	really
uh	like
basically	

We are not usually aware of our verbal-crutch habits, so you will need help in getting rid of them. If you have this problem, put signs around you such as, "Don't say *OK.*" Or tell others, "When I say *you know,* please say, '*No I don't.*'" A few days of that kind of input and you'll start to get rid of those verbal crutches.

Any obvious bad grammar is detrimental to your image. Watch out for the *ain'ts, them are, I done,* and other grammatically incorrect phrases that sometimes become a part of our vocabulary. Weed them out; they will destroy your professional image.

Slang phrases can give you a poor image as well, so get rid of those too. Some examples of today's slang: "Hey, man," "Yo," or "Man, that's really bad" (meaning it's really good).

Buzzwords are those internal phrases, acronyms, and terminology that are understood within your organization but usually not to people on the outside. These buzzwords or technical language can make others feel confused, inferior, or uncomfortable if they don't know the lingo. Without realizing it you can make others feel like outsiders, so be careful not to speak over their heads.

Words That Help

We've focused on what we should *not* say, but as we've already seen, not only can words have the power of death, they can have the power of life. We need to use more words to help and encourage, to heal and comfort, to motivate and unify.

Proverbs 16:24 says, "Pleasant words are a honeycomb, sweet to the soul and healing to the bones." Another proverb tells us, "A word aptly spoken is like apples of gold in settings of silver" (Prv 25:11). An aptly spoken word can be something as simple as a sincere compliment, a cheery "good morning," a "please" or "thank you," a "May I help you do that?" It seems today that we are often short on the simple pleasantries and good manners that were emphasized strongly not too long ago. Let's be sure to train the generations after us to use these simple, kind words and phrases. It's a good habit to instill in your children, your employees, anyone you can influence.

One way to increase your use of life-giving words is simply to verbalize the good things you already think about people. When you think, "I like her hair that way," say it. When a stranger on the elevator has a beautiful suit on, tell her. When your boss handled a meeting really well, compliment her or him. If we would just start verbalizing the positive things we think, we'd so easily become encouragers with words. I hope you'll make a commitment to do that.

Well, how would you grade yourself on your verbal skills—your choice of words? Start listening to yourself talk and see if you can discover where you need to improve in this area. The following exercise may be helpful to you.

Improving Your Verbal Skills

What words would you use for the following messages?

1. You've been asked a question you cannot answer because you don't know.

   _____

2. You have to explain to a customer that his warranty has expired and you therefore cannot repair the broken equipment without charge.

   _____

3. You have to show your coworker a mistake she made on a report.

   _____

4. You've been accused by your manager of giving a customer wrong information, but you never even talked to that customer.

   _____

Classify these phrases, using the following codes:

   D = Defensive   I = I-don't-care words
   B = Bad-news words   T = Dictatorial words (telling, not asking)
   F = Finger-pointing words   C = Condescending words

___ "Well, you can't blame me for that; I wasn't even here!"
___ "If you had just read the directions, you would have known what to do."
___ "I'm sorry; I can't help you with that."
___ "You must remember to let me know when that happens."

___ "There's no way we can get a repairman there today."

___ "As I said, all you have to do is send us the forms."

___ "Who told you that I said that? I never said that!"

___ "Put this back where you found it."

___ "I have no idea."

___ "Who's calling?"

___ "You're too young to understand."

___ "Well, you haven't been here as long as I have."

___ "I must have this right away."

___ "It's there somewhere; you just haven't found it."

What proactive words could you say in the following situations?

1. Your coworker just got a promotion.

   _____

2. You like your boss's tie.

   _____

3. A friend just lost her job.

   _____

4. Someone went out of his or her way to help you.

   _____

5. A coworker is losing weight and looking good.

   _____

6. Your manager just told you that she has been instructed to lay off three people for economic reasons.

   _____

Chapter Six

Improving Your Vocal Skills

"But, Mary," he said to me, "I'm the most enthusiastic salesperson in my office. I'm the first one here, the last to leave—I really like my job." Allen was trying to convince me that he was truly an enthusiastic person even though he didn't sound enthusiastic. In fact, he sounded like death warmed over because his voice had no inflection to it whatsoever; rather, it was a dull, droning monotone sound.

"I believe you, Allen," I said, "but I'm not your prospect on the other end of the phone. Those people do not know you are enthusiastic, and when they hear your voice, they are going to jump to the conclusion that you are lifeless and unenthusiastic about your job. That means you start with a mark against you in a business that is competitive and tough at best. Can you afford to do that, especially since your income is based on your sales record?"

You see, Allen had made the same mistake many people make, and that was to assume that he sounded the way he felt. Furthermore, when he sat through my classroom training and I pointed out the need for more enthusiasm in his voice, I could sense that he failed to see the importance of it. However, when he heard a tape recording of his conversations with some of his prospects, his eyes got wider, his mouth dropped open, and that was when he tried to convince me of his enthusiasm.

Allen had never before heard himself the way others hear him. After being confronted with the reality that he had a very unenthusiastic tone of voice, he said to his father, "I couldn't believe how I sounded in that recording. I really have a monotone voice."

"You've talked like that all your life, Allen," his father replied. Allen was shocked.

Allen learned a good lesson that day: People hear the tone of your voice before they hear your words. You can say all the right words in the world, but with the wrong voice, those words won't get you very far.

What Picture Does Your Voice Paint?

We all tend to formulate pictures of people when we talk to them on the telephone. Then when we finally meet them in person, we're usually shocked to discover they do not look like their voice.

Have you ever listened to your voice on a tape recorder? Chances are you have. What did you think? I imagine your first thought was, "That's not me!" You see, when we talk we don't hear the same sound that others hear. The sound in between our ears is very different than the sound that our listeners are hearing.

Believe me, having to listen to my own voice on the radio for over ten years has shown me how different I sound to you than I do to myself. When I first started listening to that voice on the radio, I quickly turned it off. I felt like crawling under the table. It sounded so much less sophisticated and professional than I thought I sounded. But having to listen to it six days a week, I have been highly motivated to work on my vocal skills.

Five Vocal Skills You Can Control

There are some things about our vocal skills that we cannot control. But if we will work at making sure these five things are in good shape, our voices will work for our good.

Your Voice Vitality

Does your voice sound friendly, enthusiastic, and energetic? This is by far the most important ingredient in your vocal skills. If your voice has a friendly tone to it and sounds alive, you're in pretty good shape. That will eliminate many other vocal problems (for example, you can't talk too fast and still sound friendly), and it covers up for some vocal weaknesses that we can't control.

Keep in mind that *friendly* does not mean *phony*. You've heard people who go into phony sounds on the telephone. They are attempting to sound friendly, but in the process they simply sound phony. So we're not looking for some superhype sound or some syrupy-sweet sound. Rather, we want a sound that has an "I'm a nice person" edge to it—a warmth.

Remembering what we said about needing gimmicks to change, here's one of the best gimmicks you'll find to improve your vocal skills:

SMILE!

When we smile we always warm up our sound, provided we keep smiling while we talk. You may be thinking you can't smile and talk at the same time, but you certainly can and do quite often when you're not thinking about it. The trouble is, when you start focusing on smiling in order to improve your vocal skills, you feel foolish, and you'll be certain everyone is looking at you and laughing!

That's what it feels like to get out of that rut you've been in. But remember that after a few days, that foolish feeling will go away, and not only will you have improved your vocal skills, but your face will look a great deal better because you'll be smiling more.

It's also good to note that phony smiles are as effective in warming up your voice as sincere ones. That means that even when you don't feel like smiling—*especially* when you don't feel like smiling—you just force it. Turn up the corners of your mouth and make a smile on your face. The sound will improve, and if you'll stay with it, so will your attitude.

Proverbs 15:30 reminds us that "a cheerful look brings joy to the heart." So even when your smile begins as an insincere one, it starts to affect the chemistry in your heart. You'll start to feel joy by smiling, and you certainly will make others more joyful when you smile.

The Speed of Your Speech

Do you sound rushed and hectic or relaxed and patient? All of us talk at different rates of speed, but if you generally talk in a very rapid manner, you create the feeling that you don't have time to talk to that person, or you seem unsure of what you're talking about, or you miscommunicate because others cannot understand you.

I find that many of us talk too fast at certain times:

- when we are in a rush
- when we are excited
- when we have to repeat the same thing frequently
- when we feel intimidated

You may need to slow down generally or just at certain times. Some gimmicks to use to help you are to put signs around you, especially near your telephone. Also, ask people who are around you often to give you a signal when you're talking too fast so you can become aware of it. Remember that it doesn't sound fast to you, and you will need some help to change that habit.

Of course, it is possible to talk too slowly. If people complete your sentences for you often, that's a good clue that you might need to pick up the pace. Very slow speech tends to sound uncertain and less intelligent. However, this is a much less frequent problem than talking too fast.

The Volume of Your Voice

Do you sound wimpy or intimidating? How many times have you talked to someone on the telephone and held the receiver as far away from your ear as possible because his or her voice came booming over the telephone lines? It's irritating, intimidating, and unpleasant. Interestingly, we will tell someone, "I'm having difficulty hearing you. Could you speak a little louder?" without much hesitation. But how often have you told someone, "You're speaking too loudly and hurting my ears. Could you please speak more quietly?"

If your voice is very large or very deep, you may indeed be blasting other people's eardrums, especially on the telephone, and yet you never know it because no one tells you. So check it out. Ask some people who talk to you frequently on the telephone if you come across too loudly. If so, put some signs around you and get used to talking at a lower volume. Or ask for feedback from those who work near you. Usually if your voice is too loud, your coworkers will be glad to help you change! It will take a few days to get used to that lower volume, but don't give up. It will improve your vocal skills greatly.

On the other hand, if your voice is too quiet, you will sound very uncertain and maybe even wimpy. While there are times when a quiet voice can be very effective, if you are typically too quiet, your voice probably does not have a professional, confident sound.

You will need to practice speaking with more volume, and when you do, you probably will feel like you're screaming at first. Be prepared for that uncomfortable feeling, but remember that a voice that is too quiet does not project assertively or confidently. It's worth the effort to get used to speaking with greater volume.

The Range of Your Voice

Do you sound unusually young or very authoritative? Do people call you at home and say, "Is your mother or father there?" That's a clue that your voice is probably in the upper ranges, because those ranges make us sound much younger. While we'd all like to look young, a young-sounding voice is not an asset on the job.

This is one area where I've had to work at changing my voice as I discovered that my vocal range was much higher than I realized, and I tended to go even higher when I was excited or enthusiastic. Here's the gimmick that helped me: Read out loud in your "big-bad-wolf" voice when you're by yourself and no one's listening. Remember how you read *Little Red Riding Hood* to your kids? You went into that deep range for the big-bad-wolf part. So practice that way, exaggerating your lower range and overdoing it until it starts to feel comfortable. By focusing on it and practicing, it wasn't long before those lower ranges were comfortable and much more automatic for me. And I could hear a vast improvement as I listened to my voice on the radio.

However, if your voice is naturally very low in range, be careful that it still has a friendly tone to it. A very low range without voice vitality sounds extremely intimidating and unfriendly. But a naturally low voice combined with a friendly sound is a great asset.

The Clarity of Your Sound

Are your words clear or mushy? Think about this: When you talk to someone who has very good diction, what is usually your first impression? I've asked that question of many training classes, and inevitably the answer is always "intelligent," "smart," or "educated." Good diction projects a very professional image.

Watch out for some bad habits that can accompany certain accents. We Southerners tend to clip off the beginnings and endings of our words. Here's an exaggerated illustration—a conversation between two people with poor diction (and bad grammar!). See if you can figure it out:

M R Dux

A R not

OSAR CDEDBD wangs?

L I B   M R Dux

Did you get it? Translation:

"Them are ducks."

"They are not."

"Oh, yes, they are. See the itty-bitty wings?"

"Well, I'll be. Them are ducks."

I did say it was an exaggeration, didn't I?

To improve your clarity and diction, you will need to move your lips more. Lazy lips will lead to muffled, unclear diction. And you'll need to work on any other bad habits of speech you may have.

The exercise at the end of this chapter is designed to help you identify your greatest vocal weakness and give you some practical, easy-to-do steps to correct it. Don't forget that people will hear your sound before they hear your words!

Remember: "For we are taking pains to do what is right, not only in the eyes of the Lord but also in the eyes of men" (2 Cor 8:21). True, the Lord knows you intend to sound friendly and nice, but others can't read your mind, and if your voice doesn't have a warm edge to it, you're likely to create a wrong and negative impression of yourself. We have to take pains to do what is right, and that may mean you go to the trouble to smile while you talk and work harder at improving your vocal skills.

Vocal Skills Checkup

Get a tape recorder and record yourself reading several paragraphs. Then as you play back that recording, try to hear your voice as though you've never heard it before. Candidly answer these questions about how you would perceive your voice. After you have evaluated your sound, give the recording to someone else and ask him or her to evaluate your voice using this same form. Then compare the two evaluations.

1. Did the voice sound friendly?
   ☐ yes   ☐ no   ☐ somewhat

2. Did the voice have good inflection?
   ☐ yes   ☐ no   ☐ somewhat

3. Did the voice sound lively?
   ☐ yes   ☐ no   ☐ somewhat

4. Did the voice sound sincere?
   ☐ yes   ☐ no   ☐ somewhat

5. Was the speed good, not too slow or fast?
   ☐ yes   ☐ no   ☐ somewhat

6. Was the volume good, not too loud or soft?
   ☐ yes   ☐ no   ☐ somewhat

7. Was the range pleasant, not too high or low?
   ☐ yes   ☐ no   ☐ somewhat

8. Was the diction clear and understandable?

☐ yes ☐ no ☐ somewhat

How old would you think this person is?

_____

Did this person sound like he or she really wanted to help you?

_____

Did you tend to trust this person?

_____

Did this person sound enthusiastic?

_____

Could you hear a smile in the voice?

_____

Chapter Seven

Improving Your Nonverbal Skills

"What's bothering you, Mary?" "Is something wrong? Can I help you?" "If you need someone to talk to, I'll be glad to listen."

These were the kinds of comments I received as I was walking around my college campus—many years ago! It was my first introduction to the power of nonverbal communication. Gradually, after receiving many of these kinds of comments, I realized that when I was thinking or concentrating on something, I looked worried, bothered, upset, and troubled. I didn't feel worried, bothered, upset, and troubled, but that was the message I was sending by the look on my face, the way I walked, and other body language.

All of us communicate very loudly without ever saying a word. Think about it: As soon as you see someone, you start to form a strong impression based on what you see before he or she ever says a word to you. Let's discuss a few of those nonverbal areas of communication.

How We Dress

There have been books written and seminars given about dressing for success, power ties, taboo colors for the boardroom, etc. Certainly some of it has gone too far, but there is no denying the fact that our clothes form a strong part of the first impression people have of us.

You know, I could give the same training session in my sweat suit as I can in my business suit, and I would much prefer to do that. Sweats are more comfortable. But my business audience would doubt my credibility if I did that, and they would discount any advice or suggestions I gave them because business trainers don't wear sweat suits in the classroom!

When I first started selling for IBM, there was that IBM dress code. The joke was you could always recognize IBM salespeople by the way they dressed. I decided that I needed every help I could get to meet my sales quota, and if dressing a certain way helped even a little, I was more than glad to do it. Why would I shoot myself in the foot by insisting on dressing in a nonconforming way?

Do I think we should be creative and original in our clothes? To a degree, yes. We don't all have to wear the same styles and colors. But I do believe that a real thriver is a person who understands the importance of dress and is willing to conform to what is expected in his or her job.

The code is different in different jobs, but I would urge you to go the extra mile in this area. I don't mean overdress, but do dress professionally, regardless of how others in your company may dress. Avoid severe styles, the kind that draw undue attention to you in a "Did you see what she or he was wearing?" way. Establish the look that says, "I take my job seriously, and it's important enough for me to dress right."

Here are some of my do's and don'ts when it comes to dressing. You may not agree with all of them, but before you dismiss them, at least give them some thought. Remember, we're concerned not about what we think is OK but with the impression we make on others. We're trying to thrive, not just survive, on our jobs.

Business Dress Do's and Don'ts

- Don't ever wear jeans on your job, even if they are permitted (unless you work in a physical-labor job).
- Never wear clothes that fit too tightly.
- Make sure your clothes are clean, pressed, and mended. Buttons missing, runs in your hose, wrinkled blouses or shirts, and tears in skirts or pants don't make a good impression.
- Keep your shoes polished and neat.
- Don't have your tie loosened on the job.
- Wear skirts that cover your knees, regardless of the current fashion.
- Never wear any neckline that dips too low or sags when you bend over.
- Avoid lacy, frilly clothes or any kind of evening apparel in the office.

I'm sure you don't agree with all of these, and you're thinking, "Well, it's OK where I work to wear jeans," or "All the men where I work have their ties loosened." That may be true, but it still sends a message. Think about it. We're trying to thrive here, and that means going the extra mile. You send very loud messages by the clothes you wear.

Posture

Another nonverbal communication is posture. Think of the impression you form of someone who walks with shoulders held erect versus one who looks droopy and shuffles his or her feet. Think of the impression you form of someone who sits at a desk erect versus one who is slumped in the chair. There's no question that our posture is a very loud nonverbal message.

I'm always a little surprised when I'm walking in a building, like some department stores, that has mirrors on the walls, and I get a chance to look at my posture and the image I make while walking or standing. It's not always as positive as I would like to think it is. I have a strong tendency to let my shoulders droop, and one of my objectives lately has been to correct that bad habit.

Posture is particularly important when you are in front of a group for any reason. It's helpful to practice presentations in front of a mirror or use a video so that you can see how you're coming across visually.

Facial Expressions

Your facial expressions are a very strong communication tool. Proverbs 15:30 says, "A cheerful look brings joy to the heart." Shouldn't Christians be in the business of bringing joy to the hearts of others as well as to themselves? I think so. But how many Christians pay attention to their facial expressions? It may not seem so important, but it's difficult for others to believe we have found life in Christ if our faces look like death warmed over!

This is an area God continually works on with me. When my mind is occupied with other things and I'm dashing here and there trying to get a thousand things done, I forget about how I must look to others. I'm sure many times my face sends anything but friendly messages. This is especially true in my communications with strangers—the clerks and waiters and other people I meet only briefly. So, God and I are working hard on improving this part of my nonverbal communication skills. Maybe you need some help there too.

Some important messages we can convey through our facial expressions include:

- *Sympathy and concern.* By nodding and shaking your head, as well as with your eyes and mouth, you can convey strong empathy and genuine concern. These types of facial expressions help greatly to calm angry persons and assure them that in you they have a sympathetic ear.

- *Delight and joy.* A smile costs you nothing, and it buys you a lot! Are you an easy smiler, or does it come harder for you, as it does for me? We can learn to be more natural smilers just by becoming more aware of it and making ourselves smile more often. Practice on the clerks in the stores, the cashiers at the market, the stranger in the elevator, the waiter or waitress in the restaurant. Get accustomed to smiling more often, and you will discover how powerful it is. It changes the chemistry in a conversation, both for yourself and for the other person.

- *Shock and dismay.* Your face can show disapproval through your eyes and other facial movements. There are times when it's very helpful to display dismay over a situation. It lets the other person know you are concerned, and you can say all of that with your face.

Obviously, it is also very possible to communicate the opposite of these things through our facial expressions, such as disapproval, negativeness, lack of concern, boredom, and intolerance. I remember checking into a hotel one evening, and the front-desk clerk who waited on me was not particularly efficient. As she took her time dawdling and wasting my time, I began to get irritated with her. I thought she was not behaving professionally, and I didn't think she was giving good customer service.

As I walked away from the desk to get the elevator up to my room, I was immediately convicted of my manner of communicating to her. I had not said one inappropriate word, but I had very graphically let her know, through my facial expressions, how displeased I was with her service. It was apparent that she got that message at the end, as she became very nervous. I had made her very uncomfortable—without a word!

That quiet voice within reminded me that I had one opportunity to show this person the love of Jesus through my brief communication with her, but instead I chose to show her my sour looks, my disapproving glances, and my put-upon body language. It's not enough to say the right words. We have to be very aware of the messages we're sending without words—the messages written on our faces.

Eye Contact

When you talk to someone, do you have good eye contact? That is very important. When someone does not make eye contact while communicating with you, what impression does that give you? Here are some typical reactions to lack of eye contact:

- That person is not listening to me.
- That person doesn't care.
- That person is insecure.
- That person is trying to hide something from me.
- That person is nervous.

Be sure you learn to give good, strong eye contact when you are talking to someone to avoid those negative impressions. If you find it difficult to do, practice it. I remember when I first started selling for IBM, I was scared to death. Since I was one of the first women in IBM sales, all eyes were on me, and my customers found me a novelty. So I had that added pressure, and I discovered that I had great difficulty looking my customers and prospects in the eye as I was giving my sales pitch.

This was a new problem for me, but fear and insecurity produced that negative nonverbal reaction. I'm certain my customers and prospects could easily tell how nervous and frightened I was because of the lack of eye contact. I had to consciously work at looking a person in the eye and not letting myself look away. It took effort, but I was able to correct that bad habit in a few days of concentrating on it.

Good eye contact says:

- I'm listening to you.
- I'm going to try to help you.
- I'm not frightened or intimidated by you.
- I'm confident I can handle myself and answer your questions.
- I'm honest and forthright.

Human Touch

Nothing is as strong in nonverbal communication as the human touch—a pat on the back, an arm on the shoulder, a touch of the hand. However, we must be wise about when these touches are appropriate and make certain we do not offend someone or give the wrong impression through touching.

In most business environments a handshake is the most acceptable form of this type of nonverbal communication, and you should feel free to use a handshake as a strong first and last impression. However, if your handshake is not firm, it leaves a strong negative impression. If it tends to be wimpy, practice it with some friends or family until you are comfortable with a firm handshake. Make certain you grip firmly, with your fingers wrapped around the other person's hand. Move your hand all the way into the palm of the other hand, and give an enthusiastic shake.

Let's put to rest some misunderstandings about handshakes:

- If a handshake is appropriate, it is equally appropriate for a woman as it is for a man.
- Women can and should shake hands with other women.
- Women can initiate a handshake in any situation.
- Men don't need to worry about breaking a woman's hand.
- It's totally acceptable for a man to initiate a handshake with a woman and vice versa.

Nervous or Distracting Habits

Do you have any nervous habits that could send negative messages or cause distractions? Here are some examples of these nervous habits.

- jingling money in your pocket
- doodling while someone is talking to you
- tugging at your hair
- thumping your hand or finger
- shaking your leg or foot as you sit
- picking your nose
- yawning excessively

- chewing on pencils or pens
- scratching inappropriately

Often we don't even realize that we have these habits, but they can cause perceptions that are not complimentary. Nervous habits make you appear to lack confidence or be inattentive and take away from your professional image. It's good to check yourself in these small areas because they become part of your overall image. As we've already seen, image equals perception, and perception equals reality.

Remember our verse from 2 Corinthians 8:21, "We are taking pains to do what is right." Improving our nonverbal communications skills will take pains and effort. It doesn't just happen; you and I have to work at it all the time. But it is definitely an important element to help you thrive from nine to five.

The following exercise will help you check your nonverbal skills.

Nonverbal Skills Checkup

Ask someone who knows you very well and whose opinion you value to complete the following evaluation of your nonverbal skills. (You might want to volunteer to do the same thing for him or her.) It will give you some needed input as to the impression you are making in these important nonverbal areas.

1. Do I have a ready smile?
   □ yes   □ no   □ somewhat

2. Do I look you in the eye when we're talking?
   □ yes   □ no   □ somewhat

3. Do I tend to have a deadpan expression when you are talking to me?
   □ yes   □ no   □ somewhat

4. Do you think I dress appropriately for my job?
   □ yes   □ no   □ somewhat

5. Do I have a firm handshake?
   □ yes   □ no   □ somewhat

6. Do I have any nervous habits that are distracting?
   □ yes   □ no   □ somewhat

7. Do I hold my shoulders erect when walking?
   □ yes   □ no   □ somewhat

8. Do I slouch when sitting at my desk?
   ☐ yes   ☐ no   ☐ somewhat

9. Does my style of dress draw undue attention to me?
   ☐ yes   ☐ no   ☐ somewhat

10. Does my body language and overall demeanor look confident and professional?
    ☐ yes   ☐ no   ☐ somewhat

How to Score Yourself

Questions 1, 2, 4, 5, 7, 10:
For every "yes" answer, give yourself 10 points.
For every "sometimes" answer, give yourself 5 points.

Questions 3, 6, 8, 9:
For every "no" answer, give yourself 10 points
For every "sometimes" answer, give yourself 5 points

Total Points

55–60	You have excellent nonverbal skills.
45–55	You have good nonverbal skills.
35–45	Your nonverbal skills are fair.
Below 35	Your nonverbal skills are poor.

Chapter Eight

Telephone Communication Skills

A manager in a large company had hired me to train his department in better customer service skills. He was particularly concerned with improving his employees' telephone skills. But when I called him, he answered his phone in a very abrupt tone, giving only his last name.

After getting to know him, at lunch one day I ventured to suggest that it would be a good idea if he worked on improving his telephone greeting, since we were strongly emphasizing the right way to answer the phone in the training sessions. He laughed and said, "Oh, Mary, I've answered the phone this way for years; I'm not going to change now."

I've often wondered if the training I did for his employees really made any difference. If he was not willing to work on his own telephone skills, how could he expect those who worked for him to get serious about improving theirs?

The Unique Challenges of Telephone Communication

What is your telephone image? Have you ever thought about it? You have one whether or not you realize it. Given the amount of time all of us spend on the telephone, you cannot overlook your telephone image if you really want to thrive on your job. A person who creates a consistently professional impression on the telephone is valuable to any organization and has a very marketable skill.

Consider the following challenges presented by telephone communication:

1. *Telephone communication is limited to verbal and vocal skills.* Because we can't see each other, we lose the ability to communicate nonverbally, and that, in a sense, ties one hand behind our backs. Typically we communicate many important things nonverbally. By dressing appropriately and neatly, people think of us as professional. By looking a person in the eye, we communicate confidence, caring, and listening. By smiling we are perceived by others as friendly and pleasant. With appropriate facial responses, we can let someone know we are concerned and sympathetic. Through our body language we can communicate a helpful attitude. To a large degree, we depend on our nonverbal communication skills to create a perception of confidence, sincerity, enthusiasm, and professionalism in the mind of the person we're talking to.

   However, on the telephone these nonverbal techniques simply are lost. Therefore, we must compensate for the loss of these effective communication techniques and find other ways to communicate them.

   Admittedly, some people will find it to their advantage to be able to communicate over the telephone because their nonverbal skills may be very weak. But I believe that is true for a small minority of people, and most of us are handicapped to some degree when we lose the direct impact of nonverbal communication.

2. *Many people will be far more rude, demanding, or difficult on the telephone than they would be in person.* When we don't have to look someone in the eye, we are often emboldened to say

things we would not otherwise say, so this tendency can make telephone communications more difficult.

3. *The telephone itself is a totally interruptive instrument.* How many days have you left your job thinking, "I didn't get anything done today because of the telephone"? It can ruin your schedule and plans easily. It disrupts your productivity because it causes you to stop and start all day long.

4. *The telephone is uncontrollable.* It rings when it wants to, and you can't make it fit your time-management schedule. In other words, it would be great to say, "I'll take calls from nine o'clock to eleven o'clock in the morning, then no more calls and I'll work on something else." But few people have that kind of control. It also seems to have a Murphy's Law mentality, and it rings the most on the worst days and at the worst moments!

5. *The telephone is demanding.* Even when you don't want to answer it, there is something about a ringing telephone that forces you to pick it up. Curiosity, for one thing—you never know who might be on the other end. But also that irritating ring! Not to mention that your boss can get pretty upset if you ignore a ringing phone.

6. *The telephone is impersonal.* We don't tend to form relationships as quickly or easily on the telephone as we do in person. Small talk and niceties are often overlooked when we don't have to look that person in the eye. In other words, it's easy to think of the caller as just a voice rather than seeing him or her as another person like us.

If you really intend to thrive, not just survive, on your job, you will need to recognize and overcome these unique challenges in order to cultivate a consistently good telephone image. It is a marketable skill. I would never hire someone to work for my organization unless he or she had a very good telephone voice and did a good job in relating to people on the telephone. I'm willing to pay a better salary for that skill. Many organizations have been significantly damaged through poor telephone skills.

Tom Peters, coauthor of *In Search of Excellence*, was quoted as saying, "The people answering the phones are a major competitive asset—or liability" *(USA Today*, 10 May 1994). To really thrive on your job, you need to be a competitive asset when you use the telephone.

Keep in mind that people hear your voice before they hear your words, and this is especially true in telephone communications. The tone of your voice—your vocal skills—take front and center stage here. Nothing else we can talk about in improving our telephone image will do us any good if our voice sounds rude, lifeless, or abrupt.

Improving Your Telephone Image

There are a number of things that can contribute to your telephone image. You will note that most of these are small things, but they add up to your telephone image. If you're serious about creating an outstanding telephone perception, these are the things you must do really well.

Answering Calls Quickly

It's best to answer your telephone before the third, or certainly the fourth, ring. To allow it to ring more than that starts that conversation with a poor impression.

The Telephone Greeting

By the time you've said four to five words, you've created a first impression on the telephone. When answering your phone, make certain that your greeting is first and foremost friendly and inviting. The tone of your voice should say, "I'm glad you called," not, "Why did you have to call now?" It's easy enough to check on how this sounds if you use an answering machine or voice mail of any type. Just call and listen to your recorded greeting. It may shock you to discover that though you intended to sound friendly and professional, instead you sound stiff and stilted, or rushed and abrupt, or cold and uncaring.

In a business setting, you need to make sure that your telephone greeting gives the caller needed information: typically the company name, department name, and your name. There are exceptions, of course. If the call has come through a receptionist, switchboard, or automated answering machine, you don't need to repeat the company name. If you are a receptionist or switchboard operator, you most likely don't need to give your own name, since few people are calling to speak with you and most calls are routed to someone else. However, in all other situations it is imperative that you give your name when you answer the telephone if you want to create a good impression. For you managers, this is a point on which I would not compromise—insist that your employees give their names when answering their phones.

There are additional phrases you can add to the beginning of your telephone greeting, such as:

"Good morning."
"Thank you for calling."
"Good afternoon."

Or to the end of your telephone greeting, such as:

"How may I help you?"
"How may I direct your call?" (for switchboard operators)

If you direct the call to another extension, you might add:

"It's my pleasure."
"Thank you."
"One moment, please."

However, keep in mind that callers are irritated with long telephone greetings. Typically you want to keep that greeting within three to four seconds long.

Some companies use very unusual telephone greetings to catch your attention:

"We're having a great day at ..."

That type of hyper greeting only works in very limited situations, and I would not recommend it for most organizations.

Other companies try to use the telephone greeting as a marketing tool, with phrases such as:

"Thank you for calling ABC Company,
the leader in _____."

That rarely works. The telephone greeting is not the appropriate spot to try to sell somebody something or use a marketing phrase.

There are also those organizations that insist that the people answering the telephone recite a tongue twister or give a long, complicated company or department identification. Government offices are one example of this; another is firms with multiple names. It is not realistic to expect anyone to get through four or more names every time the telephone rings. A shortened version is necessary—either the first name only or simply "law firm," "accounting firm," etc. Otherwise your telephone greeting will irritate most of your callers and give your telephone answerers many headaches!

Using the Hold Button

In an ideal world, a hold button would be unnecessary, but realistically, organizations need this feature on their phone system. Use it as sparingly as possible, and when necessary, be aware of one very important point: Don't tell; ask!

It's best to ask for permission to put a caller on hold: "Could I ask you to hold a moment, please?" Or, "Are you able to wait a moment, please?" Of course if you ask, you need to be prepared to wait for an answer. Give the caller a couple of seconds to respond. If there is no response, you can assume it's "yes"; thank the caller, and put him or her on hold. Be prepared for some callers to say, "No, it's long distance," or some other objection to being put on hold. You will need to either handle that person's call at that point, make a second request, or offer to return the call later.

On some rare occasions you may need to break this rule and tell the caller rather than ask for permission to put their call on hold. Then I would stay away from the word "hold", keep your voice very friendly, and say something like:

"One moment, please; I'll be right with you."
"I'm with another customer; I'll be with you shortly."
"I'm helping another caller, but I'll be with you shortly."
"One moment, please."

If you keep your voice very friendly without a frantic sound to it, most callers will accept this without forming a negative impression, provided you do not leave that caller on hold for a long time. But remember, this is not ideal and should be used only in extreme circumstances.

Remember that a minute on hold feels like an eternity. If you can give a caller a time estimate or offer to call back, it may save some irritation on his or her part.

Transferring Calls

Another telephone necessity that should be avoided as often as possible is transferring calls. However, it is inevitable that some callers will have to be transferred, particularly in larger organizations. It's best to stay on the line with that caller and make sure the transfer goes through properly. At least give the caller the name and extension number where the call is being transferred in case the call gets lost in the transfer process (which happens frequently!).

Some transferring guidelines:

- *Make the first transfer the last transfer!* Don't dump calls; make sure you are transferring that caller correctly. If you aren't certain, stay on the line with that caller and ask questions to confirm your transfer is correct before you drop that call.

- *Develop adequate information to allow for accurate transfers.* In many organizations, employees simply don't have the information they need to transfer calls correctly, so they guess or take a stab in the dark. A well-designed directory, showing where types of calls are directed, can be a great help in this situation. Some training of employees will make a difference as well, including adequate training on the use of the equipment. With the advanced electronics and features now available, many people have never really learned how to use the equipment correctly.

- *Take ownership of the "bounced caller."* When a caller expresses irritation or anger at being transferred several times already, you should immediately apologize for the inconvenience and assure the caller you will not transfer this call again. If you are not the appropriate person, take information and get an answer yourself or make certain the right person returns the call. Try to do some damage control with that caller by going the extra mile to help him or her.

Screening Calls

Many people use this telephone technique for various reasons. Let me begin by saying that any type of screening causes problems, and often it causes more problems than it solves. If you're concerned about your telephone image, you should hold the screening of calls to a minimum. Much screening is due to ego trips, power plays, avoiding the unpleasant but necessary calls, or postponing the inevitable. It can slow down the wheels of business and be very costly.

There are three types of screens, and I will discuss these from both perspectives—that of the person required to screen and that of the person screened.

1. Intercept screen

The screener is told to find out who is calling and why, and a decision is then made as to whether or not that caller gets through. It is the most offensive type of screen and cannot be done frequently without causing a very bad impression and creating problems. No screener can develop skills so good that he or she never irritates or upsets the caller when using the intercept screen.

If you have asked anyone to do this type of screening for you, remember that you've put that person in a very difficult position. Even if the screener's skills are very good, there will be times when the intercept screen will create bad impressions not only for the screener but for you.

If you are in this uncomfortable position of having to intercept screen, try to keep your voice very friendly, not intimidating, and ask those nosy questions as politely as possible. For example:

"May I ask who is calling and the name of your company?"
You will need both pieces of information, so ask two questions at once where possible.

"May I ask what your call is in reference to?"
This is where it gets sticky, and in all my years of business experience, I've never found or heard a really easy way to ask this question. Sometimes you can use the technique of guessing the nature of the call.

"Is your call in reference to a billing question?"
By guessing, the caller will usually confirm or give you the correct reason for the call. It can be a less offensive way to ask why a person is calling.

The most difficult situation for you as a screener is, after asking all these nosy questions, to then be told by your manager: "I don't want to talk to him or her," or, "Take a message." Now you have to find a polite way to inform the caller that the person he or she wants to talk to does not want to talk to him or her. Believe me, there is no way to completely disguise that message. The most generic response is:

"I'm sorry, she is not available."
It's true and short. If you can offer to help or offer someone else's assistance at this point, it may soften the blow.

"I'm sorry, he is not available, but perhaps I can help you."

Another bad side effect of the intercept screen is that the screener can be put in the very uncomfortable situation of being asked to lie or cover up. "Tell her I'm not in" or "Tell him I'm in a meeting" are common instructions given to screeners. Integrity should prevent anyone from knowingly lying, and there are no such things as "little white lies." Either it's truthful or it isn't. Stay with: "The person you want to talk to is not available."

If you are required to intercept screen regularly, be prepared for some rude and offended callers. No matter how nicely you try to do this, it will upset people fairly often. Furthermore, you are bound to intercept the wrong caller at some point—a spouse, brother or vice president—someone who should not be intercepted. Make certain that the person who has asked you to do this type of screening understands that it will cause problems at times.

If your calls are being screened, try to help out that middle person. Remember that he or she is only following instructions to screen calls. Don't take out your frustrations on that innocent person. Give your name, company name, and the reason for your call readily, without having to be asked. That can save a great deal of time and discomfort, and you will build some rapport with that screener.

2. Introductory screen

This is usually a far simpler screen, because the screener is asked to find out who is calling for information purposes, so the person being called knows in advance who is on the other end. The most common and best way to handle this screen is:

"May I tell her/him who is calling, please?"

This is greatly preferable to "Who's calling?" which sounds very abrupt. Remember, however, if you use the introductory screen, the caller is going to assume that the call will be put through, and it will make the caller angrier if you use this as an intercept screen rather than an introductory screen.

Often this screen is unnecessary, since the person being called does not use the information. However, it usually does not cause the kind of offense that an intercept screen can create.

3. Redirect screen

It is often necessary to redirect callers to more appropriate people. Some good redirect screens are:

"I would like to connect you with someone in our accounting department who has the information you need. I believe he/she will be able to give you a better answer."

"If you can give me an idea of the nature of your call, perhaps I can help you or put you in touch with someone who is available to help you at this time."

"Mr./Mrs. Jones would be glad to talk with you, but I think he/she would need to put you in touch with the manager of our customer service department since we don't have any records here. Would you mind if I connect you with that person now so you can have the answer more quickly?"

In the redirect mode, often the caller is trying to go to the top and may not be willing to tell you why he or she is calling. Try guessing:

"Are you calling regarding a service problem?"

Usually the caller will then either confirm or tell you the real reason for the call, and you can then redirect it to the appropriate person.

It has been reported that Bruce Nordstrom, CEO of the famous Nordstrom retailers, will accept any call from any customer at any time. It undoubtedly takes some of his time, but he can get to the bottom of any problem at Nordstrom's more quickly than anyone else. And you cannot argue with Nordstrom's success, its bottom line, or the health of its stock.

A good telephone image is critical for anyone who wants to thrive, not just survive, and that goes for any organization as well. But a good telephone image doesn't just happen. You have to do the little things consistently right. Let me reemphasize, it is the little things that add up to your telephone image. You have to be willing to take these little things seriously. It's well worth the effort, however, because few people really project an exceptionally good and professional image on the telephone. When you are able to do that, it puts you head and shoulders above the crowd.

Check your telephone image by completing the following exercise.

Telephone Image

Rate your telephone image by checking the appropriate answer for each statement.

1. I always identify myself by name when answering business calls.
   ☐ always   ☐ sometimes   ☐ seldom   ☐ never

2. I make a conscious effort to put a smile in my voice, especially on bad days.
   ☐ always   ☐ sometimes   ☐ seldom   ☐ never

3. I return all calls within one to two hours after I receive a message.
   ☐ always   ☐ sometimes   ☐ seldom   ☐ never

4. I *ask* if I can put someone on hold.
   ☐ always   ☐ sometimes   ☐ seldom   ☐ never

5. When transferring a call, I give the caller the name and number and stay on the line during the transfer, if possible.
   ☐ always   ☐ sometimes   ☐ seldom   ☐ never

6. I don't transfer a call just to get rid of it; I try to make the first transfer the last one.
   ☐ always   ☐ sometimes   ☐ seldom   ☐ never

7. When putting someone on hold, I try to give a time estimate or offer to call back.
   ☐ always   ☐ sometimes   ☐ seldom   ☐ never

8. I am aware of background noise and interfering with others who are on the telephone. I avoid talking to or interrupting a coworker who is on the telephone unless it is an emergency.

☐ always   ☐ sometimes   ☐ seldom   ☐ never

9. I refrain from chewing gum or eating while talking on the telephone.

☐ always   ☐ sometimes   ☐ seldom   ☐ never

10. When taking messages, I get name, number, date, time, and a brief message if possible.

☐ always   ☐ sometimes   ☐ seldom   ☐ never

11. When I'm away from my telephone, I inform the person covering for me.

☐ always   ☐ sometimes   ☐ seldom   ☐ never

12. When I'm upset, I make a conscious effort not to take it out on innocent callers.

☐ always   ☐ sometimes   ☐ seldom   ☐ never

Score

Count every time you checked "always."

10–12	Excellent
7–10	Good
Below 7	Poor

Chapter Nine

Five Basic People Skills

K evin had one of the best marketing minds I've ever known. His financial acumen was remarkable. He could come up with ideas and approaches that were innovative and successful. I have rarely known or worked with a person as smart as he was.

But Kevin's people skills were sorely lacking. It seemed as though he intentionally wanted to upset people and create discord. I've heard of managing through confrontation, but if that was Kevin's purpose, he failed. He simply created confrontation and alienated people. This caused disloyalty, lack of motivation, and even outright maliciousness toward him from his employees.

I often wondered, "How could any person be so smart about everything except getting along with people?" It is not an uncommon occurrence, and undoubtedly you've known some people like that too. They never really thrive on their jobs because of their inability to deal successfully with people.

In a sense, this entire book is a treatise on people skills. But in this chapter, I want to focus on five basic characteristics that make people feel very special and build respect and credibility for us.

Give People Your Attention

We all recognize the importance of giving a person our undivided attention. Let's refresh our memories on the things we can do to make sure we are doing just that.

Eliminate Distractions

It's difficult to give your undivided attention to a person when there are distractions. First, don't try to do two things at once. This is especially likely in telephone communication, where we attempt to talk and keep working at the computer, shuffling papers, or whatever else we were doing when the telephone rang. A cure for this is to start taking notes as you pick up the phone. It forces you to give your full attention to the person on the other end.

If people tend to stand around your desk and carry on conversations while you're conducting business on the telephone, find some gentle ways to remind them to move away. Hand signals, a sign on your desk, or, as one woman reported to me, a red flag you wave are some ways to send that message to move away from your desk.

If others tend to walk up and start talking to you while you are on the telephone, you can use body language to send an appropriate message, provided the phone conversation takes priority. Don't give eye contact, turn your body slightly away from the interrupter, give a hand signal indicating to wait a moment, or push a pad and pencil in his or her direction to indicate that a written message is requested. Often managers interrupt their employees in this way without considering that the telephone conversation may indeed take priority over what they have to say.

Call People by Name

It is so easy to call people by name, and it really makes a person feel very special. Don't trust your memory—write the name down when you can. Then use it several times.

When you meet someone who has a nametag on, call that person by name. When someone on the other end of the telephone gives you his or her name, call that person by name. Develop an awareness of names and use them often. It's such a simple thing to do, and it is a very powerful way to make someone feel special and important.

Give Verbal and Nonverbal Cues

Show that you are listening and therefore giving your attention by sending listening cues. In person that includes eye contact and facial expressions. On the telephone, those cues will have to be verbal—an occasional "Yes" or "I see" or something similar to indicate you are listening and haven't hung up!

Give People the Respect You Would Want Them to Give You

Nothing upsets most of us more than being treated in a condescending or arrogant manner. Be careful not to damage your career and relationships by behaving in disrespectful ways.

Bad-Mouthing and Gossip

It's so easy to get caught up in company gossip or bad-mouthing the boss or the company. Everybody seems to do it, and it almost becomes the in thing to do. You may feel you have to join in those gossip sessions to be accepted as one of the group. But that is one of the worst things you can do for your own career advancement, and in addition, it shows a disrespectful attitude toward others.

Solomon gave us some good advice: "Do not revile the king even in your thoughts, or curse the rich in your bedroom, because a bird of the air may carry your words, and a bird on the wing may report what you say" (Eccl 10:20).

Those words of disrespect have a way of getting back. You will be amazed to discover that what you said about someone in strictest confidence is now common knowledge around the office. A good rule of thumb is not to say anything about someone that you would not say to that person's face.

How do you feel when you know people have been talking about you behind your back? Do you think your boss or your coworkers feel any differently? This is one of the most disrespectful things we can do, and yet we do it so easily. If you want to save yourself a great deal of grief and really improve your opportunities to thrive on your job, make it your aim to avoid all gossip and gripe sessions.

Condescending Tones or Words

Three specific occasions come to mind where we can very easily sound condescending if we're not careful:

1. *When answering the dumb question.* Often we are asked what seems to us an unnecessary or ridiculous question. While we may give an appropriate answer, our tone of voice can carry the message, "Wow, what a stupid question!" Parents often do that with their children. Remember, while it may appear dumb to you, it obviously doesn't to the person who asks. Treat him or her with respect.

2. *When communicating with elderly people.* It may be necessary to speak a little more loudly or slowly or to repeat things occasionally when communicating with an elderly person, but it is not necessary to speak down to that person as if he or she were a child.

3. *When communicating with foreigners or people with different accents.* Typically we start to raise the volume of our voices when speaking with someone who is not as fluent in English as we are or someone who has a strong foreign accent. Remember, that

person is not deaf, but you may need to speak more slowly. Also, avoid clichés and slang in these situations, but do not use a condescending tone or attitude. I always remind myself that those people can speak two languages—one more than I can—so they certainly deserve my respect!

Develop a Reputation for Dependability

If we surveyed people who work with you, live with you, or know you well, would they describe you as a dependable person? If you really intend to thrive, not just survive, on your job, you have to be a dependable person.

A reputation for dependability is built or destroyed in little ways. If you prove to be dependable in the small things, you will undoubtedly be dependable in the big things. Here are some of those little things that matter:

1. *Keep track of any commitment or promise you make.* Do you have a method to follow up on yourself? I can't imagine that anyone can be consistently dependable without some efficient follow-up system. It can be a formal method, such as a Day-Timer, or some other sophisticated system, or a simple to-do list, as long as it works. Some people use sticky notes, but that can be dangerous because those notes can easily be lost.

   Whatever method you use, be sure to write down all your commitments and follow up on yourself consistently. If you trust your memory, you will eventually find yourself in trouble.

2. *Return your telephone calls promptly.* This is a very easy way to buy yourself a lot of credibility. Most people are amazed when someone returns a phone call promptly. It sends a very positive

impression of your professionalism, and it also tells that person his or her call is important to you.

My practice is to return the worst calls first. Whatever calls you have to make, choose the one you don't want to return and get it over with quickly. That's a good time-management technique, and it frees your mind and energizes you to get the unpleasant tasks done first.

3. *Don't promise what you cannot deliver.* Avoid the tendency to make careless promises. ("Under promise, over deliver" is a good motto.) And avoid getting caught in the trap of making a promise for someone else to deliver, such as, "I'll have him return your call." If you don't have the authority to make that happen, you've promised what you cannot deliver.

When you realize you cannot fulfill a promise or commitment you've made to someone, for unforeseen reasons, it is far more credible for you to inform that person ahead of time rather than waiting until he or she contacts you. Take the initiative to let that person know the status of the situation, even though it may not be pleasant to break the bad news.

Be Willing to Go the Extra Mile

Extra-milers are few and far between. Certainly Jesus taught us the extra-mile attitude: "You have heard that it was said, 'Eye for eye, and tooth for tooth.' But I tell you, Do not resist an evil person. If someone strikes you on the right cheek, turn to him the other also. And if someone wants to sue you and take your tunic, let him have your cloak as well. If someone forces you to go one mile, go with him two miles. Give to the one who asks you, and do not turn away from the one who wants to borrow from you" (Mt 5:38-42).

This is one of the teachings of Christ we often find difficult to assimilate on our jobs because it appears that we would just be letting others run over us and would lose effectiveness thereby. The world system is one of taking care of number one, making sure no one takes advantage of you, watching out for your rights, etc. It's not always easy to practice the extra-mile philosophy in that kind of environment.

The facts are, however, that an extra-mile attitude is a winning attitude. It's the kind of attitude that keeps customers long-term, builds long-term careers, and establishes long-term relationships. We are all impressed by people who truly do more than they are required to do.

A good approach is to look for your opportunities to do more than you have to do. Take it as a challenge to find ways to show that you are an extra-miler. Here are some ideas:

- When asked a question you cannot answer, find someone who can.
- When you're not able to do what someone has asked you to do, offer to do what you can do.
- When you see a person with a puzzled look or who seems confused, ask if you can help instead of just passing by.
- When your manager is under stress, ask what you can do to take some of the pressure off of him or her.
- With any assignment you have, ask yourself what additional input or work you could do to enhance that assignment.
- Imagine that you are the manager of your company or department and ask yourself what needs to be done. Volunteer for an assignment or, if appropriate, just do it without being asked.
- When you think you've finished a job, think of one more thing you can do to improve it.

- When a coworker is struggling with a heavy work load or deadline, offer to help.

Put Yourself in the Other Person's Shoes

Jesus gave us what we've called the golden rule, and it is still the best basis of dealing successfully with people. It's found in his Sermon on the Mount: "Do to others as you would have them do to you" (Lk 6:31). The great thing about this philosophy is that it is always a win-win attitude. When I purposely stop and try to put myself in the other person's shoes, I will of course treat that person with more consideration, patience, and kindness, and I will also reduce my own stress and frustration because I'm not thinking about me, I'm thinking about the other person.

We add immeasurable stress to our lives by being focused on ourselves and making sure we get what's coming to us. Any little infraction of our rights then causes an emotional reaction, which causes stress. However, when we are focused on other people, how they feel, why they are behaving the way they are, etc., we forget ourselves and that stress never has a chance to get started.

Are you aware of the power of empathy? Do you regularly express empathy to others? Believe me, it will make your life a great deal easier if you'll just practice empathy.

I travel a great deal, so I know what it's like to have your luggage lost. Recently I had the unique experience of having it lost twice in one week by two different airlines. In the first case, I stood in line to report my lost luggage, thinking of the inconvenience this would be for me. I would have to find a shopping center and purchase some business attire since I was dressed very casually and I had to make a business presentation the next morning. Since I couldn't count on my luggage arriving in time, I really had no choice but to be prepared for the worst.

Obviously that didn't make me happy, but I consciously tried to keep from getting upset about it. However, as I finally got to the front of the line, I said to the young woman across the counter, "My luggage did not arrive." She didn't flinch, did not look at me, simply began doing her job: asking me questions and entering a computer report. "What flight were you on?" was her first question. She showed no empathy whatsoever toward my plight, and I found myself getting angry as I stood there, wanting to unleash my anger on her. Although she was efficient in doing her job of taking the report, she was extremely ineffective in dealing with me as an inconvenienced customer. Her lack of empathy turned my slight irritation into full-blown anger and left me with a very bad impression of her and, consequently, of the airline she worked for.

Undoubtedly she would have been surprised to discover that I was unhappy with her service, since she performed the needed tasks. "What's the big deal?" might have been her response. After all, she handles lost luggage all day every day, and it is just a routine part of her job. But she failed to remember that it's not routine when it is *your* luggage that is lost, and she showed no empathy whatsoever.

Later that week I had the same experience with a different airline, but this time the woman behind the counter responded with "Oh, I'm sorry. I know how inconvenient that is." When I told her it was the second time in one week, she gave me even more empathy and insisted on checking in the back to see if my luggage had fallen off the belt (an extra-mile effort). "Sometimes that happens," she said. She didn't find my luggage, but she apologized again and assured me it would likely be in on the next flight and would be delivered to me.

I told her it was not a problem and walked away without any frustration. She did her job efficiently, but she also had enough people skills to know that while lost luggage may be routine in her day, when it's your luggage, it's a different story.

Remember, empathy goes a very long way, and you will greatly enhance your ability to get along with people by really putting yourself in their shoes and verbally expressing statements of empathy.

Use the following exercise to evaluate your people skills.

Polishing Your People Skills

This exercise will help you evaluate your people skills, and includes some practical things you can do to improve in these important areas:

1. What types of things tend to distract you when you're talking on the telephone?
   - Coworkers try to talk to me.
   - Boss tries to talk to me.
   - People stand around my desk and talk.
   - I try to do two things at once.
   - Background noise in my work environment is very distracting.

Plan of action:

- Make up a small sign, tape it to a stick or ruler, and hold it up when others are distracting you. Examples:

   "I'll be glad to talk with you as soon as I complete this conversation."

   "You can't hear my caller, but my caller can hear you!"

   "I haven't mastered the art of two conversations at once. Could you please wait until this call is finished?"

- Start taking notes to force yourself not to try to do two things at once.

- Have a private conversation with the habitual offender and ask him or her to please help you by not distracting you from important conversations. Offer to put a pad and pencil on your desk so a message can be left if he or she cannot wait.

2. Are you really good at remembering people's names?
   ☐ Yes   ☐ No

   Do you call people by name frequently?
   ☐ Yes   ☐ No

Plan of action:

Listen for names all the time; notice nametags. Write down the name when you possibly can. Make it your objective to use a person's name at least twice in every conversation.

3. When was the last time you got into company gossip with a co-worker? _____
   What led up to that gossip session?_____
   Did you instigate it or did the other person?_____
   Did you try to stop it or change the subject?_____
   Is there one particular person or people that you tend to gossip with?_____

Plan of action:

Avoid the person you tend to gossip with. Change the subject when the gossip begins. Never start any gossip; bite your tongue!

4. Is there anyone you work with or deal with whom you have thought of as not too bright? _____
   Does your tone of voice or manner of communicating tend to be condescending toward this person?_____

Plan of action:

Go out of your way to treat that person as an equal. Watch your tone of voice and your choice of words. Remember, that person is as important to God as you are, and God loves him or her as much as he loves you!

5. When was the last time you forgot to do something you promised to do? _____

    Does that happen to you often? _____

    What method do you use to keep track of your commitments and responsibilities? _____

    Would your coworkers and boss describe you as a dependable person? _____

Plan of action:

If you have no standardized, consistent method to help you remember what you have to do, start using some method today and keep experimenting with it until it works well for you.

6. When was the last time you did something on the job for a customer, coworker, or your boss that you did not have to do?

    _____

    _____

Plan of action:

List some typical extra-mile things you could do for others. Put some of them on your to-do list and make it a point to develop an extra-mile attitude.

Chapter Ten

Dealing With Difficult Types

"Why? Why? Why?" Gloria screamed at me, and without warning I found myself facing an irate person. Her accusations were bewildering, her voice was loud and high-pitched, her body language was menacing, and her self-control was completely gone. I was stunned because it caught me off guard, and I recognized this explosion needed careful handling.

I wish I could report that I did a perfect job. I'm sure I didn't. But I was able to gain my composure fairly soon, and by using sympathy over and over, I finally got Gloria to lower her voice, sit down, and regain some control.

Dealing with people who are not in control takes exceptional people skills. These may be people who are difficult for everyone to deal with all the time, or they may be people who are having a bad day or a bad moment in their day. But when they unleash their emotions on us, we are frequently unprepared and find ourselves wanting to respond emotionally. It takes strong mental and emotional control to deal with difficult types appropriately. When you do, you definitely are thriving, not just surviving, on your job.

In this chapter we will look at six types of difficult people you may encounter.

The Irate Person

A clever saying I like to quote is: "Don't wrestle with the pigs, because when you do, you both get dirty, and the pig loves it!" Now, it is not nice to refer to anyone as a "pig," so please forgive me. But you get the point. When we are dealing with an irate person, the last thing we want to do is allow our own emotions to get out of control and respond in anger. We must learn to listen well, respond correctly, but not allow that anger to destroy our objectivity or wipe out our coping ability.

Frankly, that's easier to say than it is to do, because when someone is angry at us, we have a natural tendency to respond in anger. But we can learn appropriate ways to deal with angry people so that we are successful at calming them down, solving their problems where possible, and not letting the situation get under our skin and cause us to "wrestle with the pigs."

People who deal successfully with angry or upset people are ones who use a mental "gearshift." This gearshift allows them to separate the emotion from the situation and deal with persons in a caring way without becoming angry or upset themselves. For example, an airlines ticket agent told me that her mental gearshift was to think, "They're not angry at me; they're angry at my uniform. And I take the uniform off when I finish my shift." That helped her to remember not to take people's anger personally. Others use the mental gearshift of seeing it as a challenge to try to calm the person down. These mental gearshifts are simply thought processes that enable us to keep control of our own emotions when we are dealing with someone whose emotions are out of control.

If you are able to deal successfully with angry people, pat yourself on the back! That's a great skill that will come in handy in every area of your life—on the job with coworkers, customers, and managers, at home with family, shopping as a customer yourself, and even with friends.

There are five stages to remember in dealing with a person who is irate, and it is important to follow these stages in sequence:

1. Listen and allow the person to ventilate.

Many times an angry person simply needs to vent, and once that happens, that person calms down. So when you encounter some-one—customer, coworker, manager, friend, or family member—who is in an angry state, tell yourself, "Just listen."

Often once a person gets it off his or her chest, the anger is gone and the person will talk to you in a reasonable fashion. In fact, if you allow that person to ventilate, many times he or she will end by apologizing to you or thanking you for listening.

2. Defuse the anger.

When it is your turn to talk, be sure you first go through the defuse stage. If you forget or neglect this stage, it makes your job of deal-ing with the angry person much more difficult. It may be only one sentence, but it is vital to your success in dealing with an angry per-son. Some effective defusers are:

- *Keep your voice calm and under control.* Lower the range, talk more slowly, and take the volume down. A calm voice indicates control, and the angry person will begin to bring his or her voice down to match yours.
- *Use empathy or sympathy.* This is a tried-and-true defuser that works in almost every situation. Some sample empathetic phrases are:

> "I can understand your frustration."
> "I certainly can see why that would upset you."
> "I know how annoying that can be."
> "I know what you mean; that has happened to me,
> and it can be very upsetting."

Empathy lets the person know that you hear the anger and you recognize the frustration. You don't have to approve of it, but you do need to recognize it.

You can sympathize with an angry person without apologizing. Whether or not you owe that person an apology, don't be afraid to use sympathy, such as:

> "I'm sorry you've had a problem."
> "I'm sorry this has inconvenienced you."
> "I'm sorry to hear about that."

- *Agree where possible.* When you can agree with someone, it is a very strong defuser because it takes away the "enemy" mentality. It's no longer "me against you," but you put yourself on that person's team, trying to solve his or her problem. Even if it is a small agreement, the words "I agree," or "You have a good point there," or "I can see what you mean" have a calming effect on an angry person.
- *Apologize if appropriate.* When an apology is due, it not only is the right thing to do, it also works as a very effective defuser. Few people can remain angry at someone who gives a genuine, no-excuses apology and offers to make things right if necessary.
- *Assure the angry person of a response.* It usually has a defusing effect to let this person know that you are going to respond to the situation. But, of course, don't promise what you cannot deliver.
- *If your attempt to defuse proves unsuccessful, let someone else deal with the angry person.* Many irate people will ventilate on the first person they speak with but calm down as soon as a second person comes on the scene. I call it the "second-person syndrome," and often the angry person seems to change personalities

between person one and person two. So, as a last resort, when nothing else is seeming to work, look for someone else to help.

3. Clarify the situation.

Typically, a very angry person will exaggerate the problem when speaking in anger. It may be helpful to paraphrase the situation back to the angry person, minus the anger. Often that can clear up the exaggerations and the problem becomes more life-sized.

4. Offer suggestions and solutions.

After defusing and clarifying, you should be able to go into solution stage. That will take many different forms based on the situation. It may mean you have to ask a series of questions to be able to help, investigate to find out what steps can be taken, or inform that person of the options open or the steps you can take.

I would emphasize once again, however, that you do not go to the solution stage until you've defused. So often I note that people make this mistake in dealing with angry people. They listen to the problem and the anger, and then the first words they say are something like, "Well, what's your account number?" or, "Yeah, well, first you'll have to talk to John," or "Whom did you speak with?" Those are all solution-stage questions or instructions, and if you skip the defuse stage before you begin the solution stage, it is as though you've said to that person, "Oh, big deal! Your problem is not that important." It is as though you have ignored that person's anger, and it makes for more anger.

When you are dealing with someone who has had a bad experience and is angry, please do yourself a favor: Don't skip the defuse stage! It usually requires only a sentence or two, but it can make a world of difference in the way that person reacts.

5. End on a positive note.

After you have dealt with an angry person, please remember to have the last word, and make certain that last word is positive. Say, "We appreciate your bringing this to our attention," or "Again, I'm sorry for the inconvenience," or "Please make a note of my name. You can contact me any time you have a problem," or "I'm really glad you talked with me about this."

When you have successfully dealt with the irate person, you will have a very good feeling. Keep in mind that even though you may have done your part correctly, you cannot control the response of the other person. Even if you are not able to totally calm down an angry person, as long as you stay in control of yourself and follow the basic guidelines of these five stages, you can know that you did well.

The Intimidator

You've run into this person before, I'm sure. He or she will say things like:

"What's the name of your manager?"
"I want to talk to your supervisor."
"Do you know who I am?"
"You'll hear from my lawyer."
"I'll see you in court."
"This is the last time we'll do business with you."
"I'll report this to the Better Business Bureau."
"Your boss will hear about this."
"I'm going to send a memo to the president."
"I've been here twenty years, and I know what I'm talking about."

"I know certain people in the right places."
"I have connections!"

Your first response to the intimidator is to let him or her know that you are not intimidated. You need to show a confident, calm reaction to the threat that has been made. But you must walk a very fine line here. If you go too far in showing confidence, you get into what I call smart-alecky territory. Your tone of voice, your body language, and your choice of words are very critical at this point.

The best response to an intimidator is to immediately acknowledge that he or she has the option to do whatever it is he or she is threatening to do, and then move immediately into solution stage, as though the threat is behind you. More often than not, an intimidator is bluffing and will back off quickly if you respond in this way:

"Of course you can speak with my manager. Her name is _____, and as soon as she is available, I will connect you. Meanwhile, let me see if I can resolve this issue for you."

"My manager's name is _____, and he is always willing to speak with our customers. However, if you'll give me an opportunity, I believe I can quickly resolve this for you and answer your questions. I certainly will do my best."

"If you feel that your best course is to take legal action, I'll be glad to put you in touch with our legal department (or speak with your lawyer). However, we both recognize that is not an ideal solution, and I'd like to work with you for a satisfactory resolution. Here's what we can do ..."

"You are a good customer, and we would hate to lose your business, so I'm going to do everything I can to keep you with us."

"You certainly have the right to call the Better Business Bureau; in fact, I have their number here if you would like to have it. But let me see what I can do to resolve this matter for you quickly."

Another way to show the intimidator you are not intimidated is to state your name clearly, even if you've already given it.

"By the way, my name is Mary Whelchel; you might want to make a note of it for future reference. It is spelled W-H-E-L-C-H-E-L."

That lets the intimidator know that you are confident your response has been correct and are willing to be accountable for anything you've said or done.

Most intimidators will back off rather quickly when they find someone who doesn't wilt under the intimidation, who is confident, and who at the same time genuinely tries to solve the problem.

The Whiner

Have you noticed that there are some people who seem to enjoy whining? They will repeat their problem over and over, even after it has been resolved. As soon as the current complaint is taken care of, they have another one waiting in the wings. Often they complain about problems for which there are no solutions.

When dealing with these types, you need to assume a more take-charge, businesslike approach. While speaking in a kind way, don't lay the empathy or sympathy on too heavily, but keep repeating the facts. Be prepared to be a broken record, if necessary:

"I understand, but as I said, I will be glad to send you a copy of the contract."

"Yes, I realize it has been frustrating, but as I said, we'll be glad to change our records."

"I know this hasn't been easy for you, but as I said, I will try to make certain it doesn't happen again."

You may even have to interrupt whiners, if they don't come up for air! Also, it can be effective to put the ball back in their court, so to speak, especially if they are whining about a problem for which there is no solution. Here are some ways to do that:

"Well, I'm not certain what you would want me to do. How can I help you with this?"

"I would love to be able to help you. What would you like me to do?"

This at least gets you into solution stage where you force them to either verbalize a solution or admit that there is none! Whiners can try your patience, but don't give up.

The Mistaken Person

When dealing with people who think they are absolutely, positively right but instead are absolutely, positively wrong—and you have proof—you must use a great deal of diplomacy. Don't hit them over the head with your proof; instead, find a face-saver that will soften the blow.

Rachel told me of her experience with a mistaken customer. He had called to complain that a very important order had not been received as promised, and he was not a little upset about it. Rachel promised to look into it, and when she did, she discovered a written confirmation of the order being received, two days early in fact, and signed for by an employee of the company.

With great relief and confidence, she called the mistaken customer and said, "Well, your order has been delivered. I have a shipping slip here signed by one of your employees," and she quoted the name. She was somewhat shocked when the customer said, "There's no one who works here by that name." Further investigation showed that the order was shipped to the company next door. Her proof had proven unreliable.

Whether or not you have reliable proof, it's always best to respond to a mistaken person with a face-saver to let them down slowly. Rachel would have handled this situation much better had she said, "If our records are correct, we show the order was received two days ago by one of your employees. Do you recognize this name?" This way she would not have painted herself into a corner, but even if the order had been delivered correctly, this would provide a nice face-saver for the customer.

A good principle to remember in dealing with someone who is mistaken is to find a face-saver that will let him or her off the hook. Some other examples of face-savers are:

"If my information is accurate ..."

"I'm not sure, but it looks like ..."

"I think I've got good news for you, because our problem may be resolved. If I'm not mistaken ..."

"Well, I certainly could be wrong about this—it wouldn't be the first time—but I think ..."

Keep in mind that if there is nothing to be gained by proving you are right and the other person is wrong, let it go. Lose the battle and win the war. Avoid fruitless finger-pointing as much as possible. It wastes time and energy and causes problems as well.

The Know-it-All

Have you ever met people who know everything about everything? They know more about your job than you do, and everything else for that matter. And furthermore, they have never been wrong! Often their behavior is arrogant and condescending, and they don't usually listen well.

With know-it-alls, don't expect to win. By that I mean don't expect to feel as though you resolved the issue and they are happy. They don't usually give you those good feelings. They are short on "thank you" and "please" and virtually devoid of "I'm sorry."

The best way to deal with most know-it-alls is to not get defensive and not try to win an argument. Lose the battles willingly and without anger, and go for the war. Solve the problem as quickly as you can, and then try to move on. It may also help to feel sorry for them, to put yourself in their shoes, and to imagine how difficult life must be for people who think they know it all.

Occasionally I had know-it-alls attend one of my public

seminars. From the very beginning of the session, those people would argue with every statement I made, have a different opinion on every issue, and try to discount anything I said. It used to throw me terribly, and I had a hard time just keeping the training session going. I wanted to win those battles.

I learned, however, to listen for an appropriate amount of time and then take control of my class again by either refusing to acknowledge their raised hands or turning from them bodily to the other side of the class, using body language to tell them they won't be allowed to take over my class. I keep from getting upset with them by feeling sorry for them, wondering what in the world has happened to them to make them so difficult, and feeling glad that I don't have to spend every day with them like some people do! As soon as I get in that frame of mind, they can't get under my skin any longer because I don't take their comments personally.

There were a very few times when I suggested to a know-it-all, privately at an appropriate break time, that the class didn't seem to be well suited to his or her needs. Since we had a money-back guarantee, I suggested the know-it-all would probably find it beneficial to leave the class and go back to his or her job, where he or she could be productive. That's called "drawing a line in the sand," and a know-it-all will usually either take you up on it or change his or her behavior.

The Abusive Person

Unfortunately, we've all had the very unpleasant experience of dealing with someone who becomes abusive or offensive, either through excessive and improper profanity or using words to ridicule or degrade. A woman recently shared with me that a customer said to her, "Let me talk to someone who has a brain larger than a two-year-old." That is offensive and unacceptable behavior.

As soon as a person becomes abusive or offensive, make your move. Don't expose yourself to that garbage talk; protect your mind and let him or her know it is not acceptable. The best way to do that is to give a warning, and if the behavior does not change, end the conversation. However, keep your voice calm and give that warning in a very professional manner. Here are some suggestions:

"Excuse me, but I'm here to help you, and I certainly want to help you. However, we will need to speak in normal business language. If this is not a good time for you, we can talk later."

"Excuse me, but in order to solve your problem, you will need to speak to me in acceptable language. Otherwise, I will disconnect this call."

"Excuse me, but I don't speak that language. If you want to talk with me, you'll have to use my language. If not, we won't be able to talk at this time."

"Excuse me, but I don't believe we need that kind of language in order to conduct our meeting. We can always postpone this meeting if this is not the best time."

Some companies would prefer to have this type of person passed on to a manager or supervisor, and usually the abusive person changes behavior in the process. However, I've noticed that managers and supervisors are often unavailable at these moments, so you still need to be prepared to give that clear warning.

Rarely is it necessary to disconnect or end the conversation.

Most people will change their behavior quickly, and some will even apologize to you.

If you're dealing with an abusive person face-to-face, please exercise caution. It is best to bring another person into that conversation quickly, and if you are a woman, you may want to bring a man into the situation. This is not something to take lightly. Use extra caution for your own protection.

Some wonderful verses from Proverbs give us great advice on dealing with difficult people:

A fool shows his annoyance at once, but a prudent man overlooks an insult (Prv 12:16).

An anxious heart weighs a man down, but a kind word cheers him up (Prv 12:25).

A gentle answer turns away wrath, but a harsh word stirs up anger (Prv 15:1).

Pleasant words are a honeycomb, sweet to the soul and healing to the bones (Prv 16:24).

He who answers before listening—that is his folly and his shame (Prv 18:13).

The following exercise is designed to help you improve your skills in dealing with difficult people, one of the most difficult challenges in learning to thrive from nine to five.

Dealing With Difficult People

This exercise will give you some practice on how best to respond to difficult situations. Write the first response you should have if you are spoken to in this way. (Refer back to the chapter for help.)

1. "You people make the same mistake every month. I'm sick and tired of your inefficiency. I demand you do something about this!"

   _____

2. "What do you mean, you can't get that done today? I've got to have it today!"

   _____

3. "If you aren't able to help me, then I'll speak with your manager."

   _____

4. "I'm absolutely positive you told me it was today, not tomorrow."

   _____

5. "Well, if you had good sense, you would know what to do!"

   _____

6. "I don't care what piece of paper you have, I'm telling you, that shipment has not arrived."

   _____

Chapter Eleven

Handling Criticism

Reading the mail from the listeners to my radio program is one of the joys of my life, and I still try to read every letter we receive. These letters are 99 percent encouraging and affirming, as well as very touching at times. But I remember one letter I received a few years ago. This listener wrote, "I used to like to listen to you on the radio, but I don't like to anymore. Your voice really irritates me. It sounds preachy and harsh, so I just turn the radio off when your program comes on."

A criticism—and in writing, no less, so that I had to reread it. It was actually longer and more abrasive than I've indicated, and those words hurt and sent me into react mode. I got defensive and felt sorry for myself and was ready to write her a similarly distasteful letter. However, I decided to simply ignore it and not dignify her unkind letter with a response.

The next day, however, I began to think about what she said. I thought, "Has my voice taken on a hard edge? Do I sound unkind or tough?" Certainly if you're in a radio ministry, you'd better make sure your voice is not causing problems, because listeners hear your voice before they hear your words, and if they don't like the voice, they'll do what this woman did: turn you off.

So I got some program tapes and compared some recent ones with earlier ones. You know what? She was right. My voice did sound harder and preachy. I realized that it was because of a stressful period when I was too tired and overworked, but to a listener it sounded harsh and preachy. You can be sure I made certain that problem was corrected. And I told my engineer to listen closely and if she ever heard that tone again to let me know.

Quite honestly, I have a tough time handling criticism. How about you? Reviews of my books frighten me. I have to make myself read them, because I fear they will be negative, and that would be painful. Evaluations of my presentations are hard to read because I don't want to read the negative parts. I can relate with Job who said: "Teach me, and I will be quiet; show me where I have been wrong. How painful are honest words!" (Jb 6:24-25). It seems Job had the same type of reaction to criticism that I do.

Well, it's a weakness, and it's one I must overcome because I need good, honest criticism. I need input from others so I can improve, so I can avoid making the same mistakes all the time, so I can see myself and how others perceive me more accurately. I need it, but I don't want it.

How to Handle Criticism

How would you rate yourself when it comes to handling criticism? Would your score, like mine, be on the low side? How can we improve? We don't have to be this way forever. Jesus has victory for us in every area, and that includes handling criticism.

Focus on Spiritual Growth
Handling criticism well is a sign of maturity, both spiritual and emotional. I'm discovering that as I am more and more confident of who I am in Christ and how much he loves me, the better I am able to accept criticism. As I grow spiritually with God, I also grow emotionally. Have you ever thought about that? The two go hand in hand.

Spiritual growth—knowing who God is, how we relate to him,

and how he relates to us—brings emotional growth. So I notice that as I spend time getting to know God, immersing myself in God's Word, and filling my mind with his thoughts, emotional weaknesses I see in myself begin to improve. As in every other area of our lives, the starting point for learning to handle criticism well is getting to know God better, spending time in his Word, and communicating with him regularly, growing continually in our understanding and our faith.

See It as an Opportunity and a Helpful Tool

If we're going to learn to handle criticism correctly, we've got to have the right attitude toward it. If we look at it as something negative, then obviously we'll handle it poorly. It reminds me of my first job in sales with IBM. We weren't allowed to have *problems*; we were instead faced with many *opportunities!* A positive outlook on any situation can make a huge difference in how we react.

If we can learn to think of criticism as a helpful tool in our lives that can accelerate our own growth and learning curves, then that takes a lot of the pain out of criticism and gives us a good starting place for handling it correctly. The next time criticism comes your way, send up a quick silent prayer and ask the Lord to help you see this as an instrument of good in your life. That way you can turn the pain into gain. Yes, the criticism was painful, but now you can make a painful experience a stairstep for improvement so you don't suffer for nothing. That makes sense, doesn't it?

Pray for a Teachable Spirit

We surely need to pray that God will give us a teachable heart and make us able to accept criticism appropriately. That's always a necessity for us as Christians when we recognize an area in our lives that needs strengthening. We read in 1 Corinthians 11:31 that "if we judged ourselves, we would not come under judgment." We can judge ourselves by asking God to show us our weaknesses and praying about them, and that's a lot better than waiting for someone else to judge us.

Often I pray the psalmist's prayer, "Who can discern his errors? Forgive my hidden faults" (Ps 19:12). It's difficult to discern our own errors, so we need feedback—sometimes in the form of criticism—to help us see those hidden faults and then do something about them.

Frequently, however, we do just the opposite—we bury our heads in the sand and refuse to face our weaknesses. I can think of a person who really needs some help in one of her skills. Her weakness in a certain area is very noticeable, and it wouldn't take much to correct it. However, because she can't handle any criticism, no one dares to approach her. Obviously, she is the loser because of her inability to face her own weaknesses or accept any criticism.

I understand the desire to run away from criticism—I have the same initial reaction. But I am learning to force myself to face the areas where I need improvement, and I continually ask God to show me the things that I don't see. In fact, in my prayer journal is a list of those areas in my life that I recognize to be problem areas, and regularly I bring them before God and ask him to help me become victorious in these areas. Proverbs 9:9 says, "Instruct a wise man and he will be wiser still; teach a righteous man and he will add to his learning." It's very important that we are teachable and that we continually ask God to make us more and more teachable.

Don't Get Defensive

Another good principle to learn in handling criticism is to remember to never get defensive about the criticism, even if it's unfair. Listen to it without defending yourself. That's so easy to say but so hard to do, isn't it? I know, because defensiveness is always my first reaction. But at the moment the criticism comes your way, your emotions are probably a bit out of control, and you need to wait before you speak. Give yourself time before you respond. Give the pain a chance to subside, make sure you're rested, and then consider the validity of the criticism.

I'm not saying that we should accept all criticism as valid. I am saying, however, that at the moment it is delivered, we're not usually objective enough to make a good decision about the criticism. A good response is to say very little and don't start defending yourself at that moment. I have learned that if I react right away in these types of situations, it is usually the wrong reaction. But if I wait, then I can make a fairly objective assessment and react properly.

Say "Thank You" for Criticisms

One way to handle a criticism at the time it's delivered, without allowing yourself to react at that point, is to thank that person for telling you. That buys you some time to get control of your feelings. You can always say, "You know, I really appreciate your sharing that with me. That gives me something to think about, and I will." But remember that while you're in react mode, you're not totally in control. So buy yourself some time, keep your words to a minimum, and give it some thought after your emotions have settled down.

Don't Let Criticism Send You on a Guilt Trip

We also need to learn to avoid letting criticism send us on a guilt trip. Criticisms are either valid or invalid. When they're valid, we simply need to make the necessary changes. When they're invalid, we need to get them out of our head and forget about them. In either case, we don't need to dump more guilt on our heads.

Going on needless guilt trips is self-defeating. God doesn't intend for us to be guilt ridden, and we don't have to allow criticism to inject guilt into our lives. Once you have assessed the criticism, objectively faced the issue, and taken whatever corrective action necessary, the guilt should go. Often we have the tendency to keep dwelling on the criticism after it's been taken care of or when there is nothing more that can be done. That's counterproductive and keeps us mired in false guilt.

Solicit Helpful Criticism
Another good thing is to learn to solicit criticism when appropriate. A good sign of maturity is recognizing you don't know it all and asking the appropriate people to give you some constructive, helpful criticism. Of course, you need to know that the person has your best interest at heart and is capable of giving you good advice in that area, but don't just ask people who will say only good things to you. If you really want to improve in some area, solicit good criticism from the right people. It's easier to handle criticism when you solicit it, and usually it is given in a more palatable form.

Learning to Give Criticism

When it is your job to offer constructive criticism, ask God to give you discernment about that person. Different people handle criticism very differently, and we need to be sensitive to their feelings. However, when it is our duty to deliver a needed criticism, we must be willing to do it even if that person has an initial reaction of defensiveness or nonacceptance. Even if he or she never changes, we should not neglect our responsibility to offer the criticism, in the kindest way possible, for his or her good.

However, when it's not our job to offer constructive criticism, we need to learn to keep our mouths shut and allow people to learn through their own mistakes. Parents can have trouble with this, especially as children grow up. Recently Barbara told me that her grown daughter and son-in-law felt she interfered in their lives too much and was too critical. Barbara said to me, "I just want to help them, and when I see them making a mistake, I try to give them good advice." But they were perceiving it as criticism and interference.

I told Barbara, "Just pray and keep your mouth shut." Rather abrupt advice, I realize. But there is a time when you need to back away, let your grown children make their own mistakes, pray a lot for them, and give advice and criticism only when asked. Obviously, if you have a child walking in paths of sin and destruction, God may lead you to give a warning. But even then, in the end the decision is still the child's.

Remember that if you're on the receiving end of a criticism that is delivered poorly, you'll do yourself a great favor by making every effort to hear the criticism and not let the delivery get to you. Separate the form from the content. Look beyond poor delivery for relevant feedback, and you may discover some very meaningful information to help you.

I like warm fuzzies a lot better than criticism, but I need honest criticism. Without it my growth and effectiveness will be diminished, and I don't want that.

Proverbs 19:20 says, "Listen to advice and accept instruction, and in the end you will be wise." And in Proverbs 13:18 we read, "He who ignores discipline comes to poverty and shame, but whoever heeds correction is honored." We need to put a discipline into our lives that allows us to handle criticism correctly. We are the winners when we do, and we'll thrive, not just survive, on our jobs with that kind of attitude.

Use the following exercise to find areas where you could improve the way you handle criticism.

How Do I Handle Criticism?

Evaluate your ability to handle criticism appropriately, identify your weak areas, and make a plan to improve:

1. When someone criticizes me, my most common reaction is:
   - ☐ I go on a big guilt trip, though often I don't know why I feel guilty.
   - ☐ I immediately defend myself verbally, usually angrily.
   - ☐ I strike back at the person who has criticized me and try to make him or her feel bad.
   - ☐ I clam up, say nothing, and pretend it hasn't happened.
   - ☐ I get my feelings hurt and sulk.
   - ☐ I try to undermine that person behind his or her back and destroy his or her credibility with others.
   - ☐ I try to control my reaction, get past the hurt, and consider the validity of the criticism.

2. I have the greatest problem with the following types of criticism:
   - ☐ Criticism from someone I don't respect.
   - ☐ Criticism from someone who is much more in need of criticism than I am.
   - ☐ Unfair criticism for which I'm not guilty or responsible.
   - ☐ Criticism given in the presence of others.
   - ☐ Criticism given in anger.
   - ☐ Nonconstructive criticism given to harm, not to help me.
   - ☐ Criticism of me in a certain area (such as job performance, appearance, dependability, attitude, motives, etc.). Identify that specific area:_____
   - ☐ Criticism given at the wrong time, when I'm tired, frustrated, overworked, or depressed.

3. It is most difficult for me to handle criticism from:

Why?

☐ My manager   _____

☐ Coworker(s)   _____

☐ Customer(s)   _____

☐ Spouse   _____

☐ Children   _____

☐ Parent(s)   _____

☐ Specific friend(s) _____

4. I have honestly asked the following people to offer me help, advice, or a critique in an effort to improve myself.

What/When

☐ My manager   _____

☐ Coworker(s)   _____

☐ Customer(s)   _____

☐ Spouse   _____

☐ Children   _____

☐ Parent(s)   _____

☐ Specific friend(s) _____

5. When I criticize others:

☐ I only do so when it is appropriate (i.e., when it's my job, that person is my responsibility, or that person has solicited my help).

☐ I never criticize someone in the presence of others.

☐ I try to affirm the person with positive feedback at the same time.

☐ I try to make certain that I am doing it for the other person's benefit, not just to vent my anger or frustration.

☐ I think ahead of how I will phrase it so that my words are as gentle as possible. I try to speak the truth in love.

☐ I keep my voice calm and controlled.

☐ I try to find a time when the other person is not rushed, tired, or otherwise distracted or frustrated.

6. These are the areas where I need to improve in handling criticism:

☐ Stop being so defensive when I am criticized.

☐ Learn to listen to the criticism, ignore the emotions, and turn the *pain* into *gain*.

☐ Not allow an overly critical person in my life to continually send me on guilt trips.

☐ Get through the react stage and make myself consider the validity of the criticism.

☐ Stop trying to get back at the person who criticizes me.

☐ Stop criticizing others when I am not the right person to do so or it is not the right time.

☐ Learn to mentally let go of the criticism once it is over.

Chapter Twelve

Managing Your Time and Work

She worked very hard; she stayed late every evening; she hardly ever took lunch breaks; she always seemed overwhelmed and overworked. She was working so hard that she generated a good deal of sympathy. "Poor Susie, I feel so bad for her. She has so much to do and never gets out of here on time." Those were typical comments her coworkers made about her.

I was one of those coworkers, often feeling guilty myself for not working as hard or as long as Susie did. However, after getting to know the situation better, I began to see that Susie did indeed work long hours and expended a great deal of energy, but many of us were accomplishing the same amount of work in much less time because Susie did not use any discipline in planning her work, scheduling her time, or controlling her energy.

Sometimes I even got the idea that she was trying to solicit those expressions of sympathy. It made Susie feel good about herself to be able to say how late she worked last night, to remind us that she didn't have time to go to lunch today, to be there at the office every morning before the rest of us. I concluded that Susie was doing this in part to convince herself that she was important and valuable.

Many times in my career I've worked with people who worked hard but not smart. People who really thrive on their jobs are ones who know how to use that eight- or nine-hour day really well, completing assignments and keeping up with the work in a fairly normal schedule, leaving time for the rest of their lives and achieving a balance in lifestyle.

Have you heard the slogan "Plan your work and work your

plan"? I remember having that drilled into me early in my career, and there's an awful lot of good advice wrapped up in those few words.

Time is our most valuable resource—the one we can never replace once we use it. God will hold us accountable for our use of time. We've each been given twenty-four hours each day, but some use those hours more wisely than others.

Paul told the Ephesians they should "be careful how you walk, not as unwise men, but as wise, making the most of your time, because the days are evil" (Eph 5:15-16, NASB). We need to learn practical ways to make the most of our time, and in so doing, be approved by our Lord as wise servants.

Time management is a topic that has been covered in depth by many other people, yet few of us really manage our time well. Certainly we cannot say it is from lack of information or help, because most any bookstore or library is a resource for good help in how to plan your work and work your plan. Mostly it's a matter of just making up your mind to do it.

However, I've discovered that some people really have no concept of what they need to do in order to get the most out of their twenty-four-hour days. So here are some practical ways to make good use of your time—whether it's on your job or in your personal life.

Become Goal-Oriented

Do you know the difference between a wish and a goal? A goal is something that is realistic and achievable. I could wish all day that I could be an astronaut, but that could never be a goal because it's not achievable for me. A goal has a time schedule and is measurable in some way or another. I may wish to lose weight, but in order to do that, I need to set a goal and a time frame for that goal. "I will lose ten pounds in four weeks." That's a goal.

Given that definition of a goal, are you truly a goal-oriented person, or do you just wish a lot? I find many of us are very good wishers, but not many of us take those wishes and turn them into goals that we work to achieve. After all, wishes don't take any energy or discipline; goals do. Wishes don't require any commitment from us; goals do. Here are some examples of wishes and how they can be turned into goals:

Wish	Goal
I want to be more organized.	In order to be more organized, I will start using a to-do list on a daily basis beginning today.
I want to get along better with my co-workers.	In order to get along better with _____ (specific person), I will invite her to have lunch with me next week and try to develop a better relationship with her.
I want to get out of debt.	In order to be a better steward of my money, I will pay off all credit card accounts before charging anything else, and then I will only charge what I can comfortably pay off each month.
I want to find a more interesting job.	In order to find a job that interests me more, I will take a course in computer skills beginning in January at the local community college to get the education needed for advancement.

Think of one thing you want to achieve—one thing you want to improve in your life, on your job, or in your relationships. Write it down. Now ask yourself, "Did I write a wish or a goal?"

Once you've written it down and gotten it into the form of a goal, ask yourself, "How much do I want this?" If you're not truly committed to achieving that goal, it simply won't happen. Jesus said we find God when we search for him with our whole heart. Lots of people would like to know God better, but few are willing to put out the time and effort required to search for him with the whole heart. As you look at your goal, you have to be certain you are truly committed to it.

To become a goal-oriented person, you must list your long-term goals, list your daily short-term goals, divide your goals into manageable portions, and make yourself accountable.

List Your Long-Term Goals

First, sit down and make a list of the long-term things you want to do, both job-related and personal. Most of us have dreams and plans of things we're going to do "when we have time," but somehow a lot of those things never happen because we keep running out of time. Often they are the really important things that should be done. If you don't plan to put them into your daily schedule, they'll never happen.

So list all those things you want to do. Perhaps it's "take a course in writing skills," or "rearrange the filing system to be more efficient," or "take a Bible correspondence course." Once you've listed those long-term goals, prioritize them, and set a deadline for each one. Be realistic about those deadlines, but you need to put some time frames in place.

List Your Daily Short-Term Goals

Now, make a second list—your to-do list of things that are on the schedule for today. I strongly encourage you to work with a list each day. You don't have to spend lots of time making the list—a few minutes should do it—but it is very helpful in keeping you on track through the day.

In order to get those long-term goals accomplished, you have to put parts of them on the daily to-do list. So each day try to do at least one small part of a long-term goal. Maybe you can only devote fifteen minutes to it, but if you keep on, you'll start to chip away at those long-term goals you never seem to get around to doing.

Remember to include on your list things like, "Write a note to Barbara to encourage her," "Send a card to Jane for her birthday," and "Call Sue and invite her to church." If you don't, they'll frequently get lost in the shuffle.

Divide Your Goals Into Manageable Portions

In order to achieve those larger goals, make sure you bite off small pieces at a time. Sometimes we discourage ourselves because we see the job before us as so large that it looks like we'll never make it. But if we take the large goal and turn it into a series of small ones that don't look impossible, pretty soon we'll find we've achieved our goal.

This is the sixth book I've written. Each one seemed an impossible goal at the beginning. I was overwhelmed and discouraged. But each time I turned that big goal into a series of small ones, setting deadlines for each chapter, each section. I could tackle writing a chapter but not writing a book. But after writing thirteen or fourteen chapters, I have a book! That's one of the most important principles in setting realistic, achievable goals: Divide them into small sections that don't overwhelm you.

Make Yourself Accountable

I would encourage you to establish accountability for yourself in these goals that you set. Ask someone to check up on you. Let some people know what your goals are. That accountability is very important.

Setting goals is a technique that works in all areas of our lives. As we become goal-oriented people, we will be pleasing to our Lord for we will become increasingly better stewards of the time and resources he has given to us.

Internal and External Prime Time

One way to manage your time better is to be aware of your internal and external prime time. Internal prime time is that time when you work best. For me, it's 5:00 A.M. to noon. I'm running at highest capacity then; my energy is high, my drive is high, my creative juices are flowing. As much as possible, I save my prime time for time with God and for writing.

It's easy to let your prime time slip through your fingers, eaten up with telephone calls and incidentals that could be done in non-prime time. I always try to schedule appointments outside my office in the afternoon if I can. My staff is very helpful in keeping interruptions away from me during the morning hours. I try to push tasks that are not as mentally demanding into afternoon and evening time, when I slow down.

As much as possible, use your internal prime time for your most important tasks—the ones that require the most energy and creativeness on your part.

External prime time is when external resources—usually people—are most readily available for decisions, inquiries, and information. Make telephone calls when you have a high probability of getting through to that person. Learn the best times to catch your boss for those needed times of interaction. When are you most likely to find office equipment available? Plan your duties to eliminate as much waiting time and telephone tag as possible.

Plan for Interruptions

Unexpected happenings take time, and I seriously doubt we ever have a day that isn't interrupted at some point or another. We certainly have to plan to be flexible as we plan our work and work our plan. But starting out with a plan, even if it gets changed, is still the smart way to manage your time and make the best use of it.

Simplify and Unclutter Your Environment

What does your desk or your work surface look like right now? Is it totally cluttered and covered with stuff? Do you hang on to things too long? How often do you just reshuffle things that need to be done? Is your desk or work station loaded down with papers and projects that you keep rearranging, refiling, relisting on your to-do list? If you added all the time you spend shuffling the papers, you could have accomplished many of the tasks while you were rearranging the papers!

Sometimes I have to stop and make a high priority of getting rid of the projects that are sitting on my desk and gumming up the works. As you reshuffle papers, ask yourself, "Why should I not do this right now?" If you can't think of a good reason, and if it truly has to be done, then get it off your mind, off your desk, out of the reshuffle mode. "Handle each piece of paper only once" is a good rule to follow. If it can be done now, do it now.

Procrastination—a Deadly Habit

Of course, sometimes we go in the other direction and keep ourselves busy doing low-priority items in order to avoid facing the more difficult and demanding priorities. Perhaps you just don't know how to begin one of those projects on your list, so you've been keeping busy doing a bunch of little stuff to avoid facing it.

I have learned that the only way to start is to start. Just jump in with both feet, over your head, and start swimming!

Procrastination is a deadly habit. How many things do you have lined up to do that you just haven't started? I encourage you to do something today that makes a start on the project. Make a telephone call, ask a question, write the first page—*start*. That's frequently the hardest part; if we don't *start*, nothing will ever happen.

Learn to Say *No*

A good time manager is one who knows how to say *no* when appropriate. I have to admit that I find it difficult to say no, but I'm learning.

Just because you're asked to do something doesn't mean you necessarily are the right person to do it. Don't be pressured into saying *yes*. Be careful of saying, "I'll do it right away," when you know you can't.

If your boss asks you to do something you feel is not the best use of your time, you could say something like, "I'll be glad to do that for you now, but if I do, I won't be able to complete this other project you gave me yesterday. It was my understanding that it had a higher priority. Is that right?"

When people say, "Do you have a minute?" they usually want much more than a minute. You could ask, "Are you serious about one minute? I have a minute now, but if it takes longer, we'll have to do it later."

Minimize Interruptions

Who interrupts you the most? How can you minimize those interruptions? Perhaps you can suggest to that person that the two of you can confer at specified times and try to cover all that needs to be covered at one sitting instead of those multiple conversations that interrupt your work flow and eat up so much time. That would be a great timesaver.

Group activities together to avoid start-up time. Instead of writing a few checks every day, for example, write checks on Friday. You'll eliminate a great deal of start-up time.

Set some routines in place to avoid delays and harassment. For example: Are you always running out of needed supplies and inventory? Set up a routine and a checklist that forces you to check all supplies on certain days or turn in an order form when supplies are low. This will help you avoid those panic moments when you're trying to locate what you need. It can save lots of time and hassle as well as money.

Give God the First Fruits of Your Time

Let me conclude these thoughts on time management by reminding you to reserve a key part of your prime time each day to spend with the Lord, reading his Word and praying. Every Christian should have that at the top of his or her to-do lists.

It seems as though we have a hundred good reasons to skip that time with the Lord, and so many things seem to get in the way. But I can tell you from firsthand experience that if you try to operate without quality and quantity time with God each day, you are handicapping yourself.

If you'll spend time with God at the beginning of each day, you're going to discover that the rest of your day will be much more efficient and productive, much less hassled and frantic. Believe me, you cannot afford not to make that your highest priority.

I believe much of our frustration comes from poor use of our time. It causes confusion, it makes us feel like failures because things don't get done, and it adds much stress to our lives.

Remember Ephesians 5:16: "[Make] the most of your time, because the days are evil" (NASB). It may not seem like a spiritual function to plan your work and work your plan, but indeed we honor the Lord when we make the very best use of what he has given us—time.

Use the following exercise to evaluate your time-management skills.

Time-Management Checkup

Find out how you rate as a time manager by checking the most appropriate response to each statement.

1. Most of my days begin in a calm fashion because I get up early enough to avoid rushing.
   ☐ always ☐ usually ☐ sometimes ☐ never

2. I use a daily time-management technique to keep track of what needs to be done, and I set priorities.
   ☐ always ☐ usually ☐ sometimes ☐ never

3. I am not late for appointments, work, or other commitments.
   ☐ always ☐ usually ☐ sometimes ☐ never

4. My assignments are completed on schedule.
   ☐ always ☐ usually ☐ sometimes ☐ never

5. I have some specific long-term goals that I am working on consistently (work-related or personal).
   ☐ always ☐ usually ☐ sometimes ☐ never

6. I do not keep shuffling and reorganizing the papers on my desk but regularly go through and clean it off.
   ☐ always ☐ usually ☐ sometimes ☐ never

7. I use a filing system to keep track of needed information and paperwork.
   ☐ always ☐ usually ☐ sometimes ☐ never

8. I am not a habitual procrastinator, and I try to avoid the last-minute crisis mode.

   ☐ always ☐ usually ☐ sometimes ☐ never

9. I can get my job done in the allotted time without undue overtime. (If you are working overtime often, determine if it is truly due to an unrealistic work load or because you don't work as smart as you could.)

   ☐ always ☐ usually ☐ sometimes ☐ never

10. I can juggle any responsibility that I have and don't lose track of what I'm supposed to do and where I'm supposed to be.

    ☐ always ☐ usually ☐ sometimes ☐ never

Score

Count every time you checked "always."

9–10	You're an excellent time manager.
6–8	You're a good time manager.
4–5	You have much room for improvement in your time management techniques.
2–3	You have a poor record of time management.
0–1	Help!

Chapter Thirteen

Controlling the Controllable

Marsha is a Christian woman I admire who was faced with an uncontrollable situation—a workaholic husband. She had tried through many years of marriage to Scott to get him to break his bad workaholic habits, but to no avail. Finally Marsha came to the conclusion that she could not control Scott; she could not force him to change; she could not make him listen to her.

At that point Marsha had a decision to make: Become a nag, or leave Scott and ruin both of their ministries, or control what she could control and find her fulfillment in legitimate ways apart from her husband, since he was rarely there for her and was completely occupied with his activities. Marsha made a decision not to abandon her marriage or her family but to control what she could control—herself. She became involved in things that fulfilled her and used her gifts and talents, doing things that brought her satisfaction and ministered to others. While she would have preferred to have Scott involved with her, Marsha could not control him, so she controlled what she could control—herself.

Eventually Scott became aware that Marsha was finding fulfillment in other activities. When he said to her, "You are no longer delighting in me," she was able to gently point out to him that it was true; she was finding fulfillment in areas where he was not involved, but only because she had not been able to convince him that his workaholism was a problem. With Marsha's loving help, Scott was then able to see her point. He began a project to overcome his workaholic habits, and now he has dramatically changed that situation.

I was impressed and challenged with Marsha's approach to her problem. She could have handled it in a very destructive way, but instead she chose to control what was in her power to control—herself—and not waste any more time or energy trying to control what she could not control—her husband. But Marsha did it in such a loving, nonselfish way that eventually she was able to help Scott see his problem, and then he was willing to control what he could control—his workaholic tendencies.

I read something recently that really caught my attention: If you can control the controllable, you can cope with the uncontrollable. I started to think about that and realized how true it is.

Don't you think we often spend a lot of time and energy fretting about things that are beyond our control? We try our best to control those uncontrollable people or things, manipulating here and there, discovering in frustration that our efforts are futile. Thriving, not just surviving, depends in great measure on our ability to focus on the controllable and learn to let go of the uncontrollable.

Those uncontrollable things in our lives may not be directly associated with our jobs, but any time we try to control the uncontrollable, it will affect all areas of our lives in a negative way. You may be trying to control an uncontrollable family member, but that will have a ripple effect in your ability to handle your job because of the emotional drainage it causes.

Facing the Uncontrollables

Four of the most common uncontrollables in our lives are other people, our heritage, our past, and our environment and circumstances.

1. Other People

Marriage Partners. My mail often brings stories of a husband who left after twenty-five years of marriage, or a young wife who suddenly decided she wanted to do her own thing and not be tied down to children or a husband. In my Sunday school class there are at least six women who are living with husbands who need changing—alcoholics, unbelievers, difficult personalities—but through many years of marriage, they have not been able to change these men.

Or perhaps it's something as small as trying to change your spouse's habit of throwing dirty clothes on the floor or forgetting to put the cap back on the toothpaste. All married people have some frustration at not being able to control their spouses.

Children. Parents have to face the reality that you cannot always control your children. As tough as the terrible twos can be, at least you can pick up a two-year-old and control his or her actions through physical restraint if nothing else. But as they grow older, you realize how often you are helpless to control the behavior of your children. Some of you have children who are now drug-dependent, alcoholics, living in sin, or walking away from their Christian upbringing. You can talk, you can cry, you can even pray earnestly, but you cannot by yourself control that child who now has the freedom to behave as he or she pleases.

I think of Deborah, a dear friend who is patiently trusting God to bring her sons back to her. They were raised in a Christian home but have chosen to abandon their faith. For many years Deborah's sons have lived lifestyles foreign to Christian beliefs, and she longs to see them change and come back to God. She will never give up hope nor will she quit praying, but the facts are, she cannot herself control their behavior. If she could, they would have long ago changed and would now be living for Jesus.

Bosses and Coworkers. How many times have you said something like, "If my boss would just be more organized," or "If my manager would just communicate better," or "If only I didn't have to work for such a tyrant!" You've got a boss you'd change in a minute if you could, but you cannot control your boss—right?

The same is true for your coworkers. Rebecca has worked for over two years with Helen, a woman who is pretty close to intolerable. Helen makes every day on the job a difficult and unpleasant experience. Believe me, if Rebecca could change Helen and control her words and actions, she would. However, Rebecca has learned to accept the fact that she can never control Helen's behavior.

2. Our Heritage

You had absolutely no choice about the family you were born into. You just opened those baby eyes, and there you were in this big world with some people you got to know really well. I was highly blessed to be born into the most wonderful kind of family with lots of love, security, and Christian upbringing. But I'm well aware that many of you had family situations that were—and possibly still are—painful and difficult. That can range from simple personality clashes to abuse of all kinds.

We could not control whether we were born boys or girls. The family we were born into is beyond our control. Our heritage from that family is not controllable.

3. Our Past

Some of us would like to change something about our past. The sins and mistakes, the bad decisions, the wrong turns—they haunt us, and we often imagine what life would be like if we could just control that past.

I think of Nancy, a Christian friend who married a man she knew was not a Christian. She was well aware of the potential problems but chose to marry him anyway. After many years of marriage, Nancy has had to learn to cope and live with the situation because she cannot now control or change that bad decision she made that has affected her entire life.

You know, there's not one thing you or I can ever do to change our past. It's already in the books. As painful or as difficult or unfair as it may seem, you cannot control your past any more than you can control your heritage.

4. Our Environment and Circumstances

There are certainly many environmental things in life that are not controllable: the economy, the company's decision to downsize, the drunk driver who swerved and hit your car, the cost of living, taxes, company policy, the weather—the list goes on and on.

Our Typical Response to the Uncontrollables

What do we typically do when we encounter the uncontrollable people and things in our lives? Frequently we try to change them, to gain control. How many wives have tried to change their husbands and vice versa? It seems almost every couple goes through that tension of trying to change each other. We try to change our children, our parents, our coworkers, or our bosses because we're totally convinced that if they would change the way we want them to, life would be so much better for everyone. That may be true, but they aren't that easy to change, are they?

Another way some people respond to uncontrollable people or situations is to live in denial and pretend they don't exist. Or some try the runaway method. I think of Irene, who moves a lot, changes jobs frequently, can never find a church she likes, and is always on the run. Her method of coping with the uncontrollable is to run away from the problem.

Who hasn't tried that method at some time? David put words to our runaway tendency when he wrote, "Oh, that I had the wings of a dove! I would fly away and be at rest" (Ps 55:6).

Consequences of Trying to Control the Uncontrollable

When we live in that mode of trying to control the uncontrollable, we almost always end up in frustration and disappointment, and we do ourselves great harm. We build up anger and bitterness that damage us greatly. We become vindictive and vengeful, and we add immense stress to our lives.

Can you even begin to think of the time, energy, and emotions you've wasted on the uncontrollable things in your life? I've certainly done my share of wishing, fretting, complaining, and trying to manipulate uncontrollable things and people. When I do that, I use up immense quantities of emotional energy for nothing when it could have been expended in a productive way. I'm in survival mode then—not thriving, just hanging on for dear life!

Also, when we are trying to control the uncontrollable people in our lives, what we are actually doing is allowing them to destroy our joy. Discovering that we cannot control them, but continuing to try, we are at their mercy. Our happiness, peace, or contentment depend on their behavior, performance, or attitude. We find ourselves on an emotional roller coaster—up when they are behaving well and down when we can't control their behavior.

Then when we are frustrated because we can't control the uncontrollable, we tend to take it out on the Lord. Our fellowship is broken, and we suffer greatly because we don't have his love and strength to help us. Why do we do that? God didn't fail us, leave us, or forsake us. He wants to give us peace that passes understanding. When we don't have that peace, it's because we have forsaken him, not vice versa.

It's hard to learn not to try to control the uncontrollable. Recently I had to deal with a truly uncontrollable situation, and I desperately tried to bring it under control. I was frustrated, couldn't sleep well, and couldn't function nearly as productively as usual because I was so consumed with trying to fix what wasn't fixable.

Finally I heard that inner voice of God's Spirit saying, "You will never be able to tie a bow on this package," meaning no matter what I did, the situation would not improve. So I had to let it go without a solution, without an ending, without a "happily ever after." That's very hard for me to do.

You, too? Oh, but those times teach us to trust in our heavenly Father. They teach us to recognize how weak and helpless we truly are. They teach us humility, faith, and dependence on God.

Remember this: When the uncontrollable things or people in our lives are making us miserable, it is because we *allow* them to do that to us. They can't keep us on that roller coaster if we decide to get off. How do you get off? By choice, by a decision of your will, by much prayer, and by the power of God's Spirit within you. It takes determination on your part, but if you don't let God supply the power, you're not likely to be able to do it.

Finding Freedom From the Uncontrollables

What are you facing in your life right now that is uncontrollable? There is undoubtedly something or someone—maybe more than one. How have you been coping with that uncontrollable thing or person? In fear, frustration, anger, or despair?

Well, I have great news for you. If you focus on controlling the controllable, you will be able to cope with the uncontrollable. You do not have to continue to be a prisoner of the uncontrollable things and people in your life. Jesus Christ has come to set you free from all prisons, and he is totally capable of doing just that.

Are you willing to let go of that uncontrollable thing or person? To admit you cannot control or change it? Are you tired of living in denial or trying to run away? Are you ready to forsake the bitterness and vengeance that has built up over the uncontrollable thing or person? It all begins in your mind and in your will.

God is able and ready to take that uncontrollable thing or person and carry the burden for you. Whether or not it ever is resolved, he is there to give you all the help and support you need. God won't move in until you confess that it is beyond your control.

Acknowledging the Controllables

There are things in our lives that we can control. They include our relationship with God, our thoughts, our tongues, our attitudes, and our integrity. Let's focus on the controllables.

Our Relationship With God

We are as close to Jesus and our heavenly Father as we want to be. It takes commitment, discipline, and desire, but he has promised that if we seek him with our whole heart, we will find him. Are you controlling your relationship with Jesus? When your relationship with Jesus is more important to you than anything else, you have the strength to cope with the uncontrollable.

If you're like me, you find that when you're struggling with the uncontrollable, the first thing you start to neglect is your relationship with Jesus. Either you excuse yourself because the uncontrollable thing or person is taking so much of your time, or you just don't feel in the mood. Trying to control the uncontrollable is very frustrating and leaves us emotionally depleted, doesn't it? So we just don't have any desire to spend time with Jesus.

No one can keep us from having a close fellowship with Jesus if we want to. Think about that. There is no person or circumstance that can rob you of Jesus. Paul told us that, and he really pulled out every word in his vocabulary to get this point across to us: "For I am convinced that neither death nor life, neither angels nor demons, neither the present nor the future, nor any powers, neither height nor depth, nor anything else in all creation, will be able to separate us from the love of God that is in Christ Jesus our Lord" (Rom 8:38-39).

Paul was referring to our eternal security as believers, but he was also referring to our daily walk with the Lord. Nothing and no one can interfere with our ability to experience and know the love of Jesus in our lives if we don't allow it. The world can lock us in prison and take away everything we own, but nothing can take away Jesus and his presence in our lives.

Is that uncontrollable thing or person in your life right now coming between you and Jesus? It doesn't have to be that way. You can make a choice right now, that regardless of how difficult or frustrating the uncontrollable is, you are going to stay closely attached to Jesus Christ. That means getting back to spending time with him, feeding on his Word, talking about him, and thinking about him, instead of focusing on the uncontrollable.

I promise you, when Jesus is the central focus of your life, the uncontrollable takes on a whole new perspective. While I spent those frustrating days trying to control the uncontrollable, worrying about the situation, and wasting precious time and energy on what I could not control, my desire to spend time with Jesus went downhill because I was emotionally so exhausted over the uncontrollable thing.

Finally one morning I got back to my time with the Lord, and as soon as I opened the Word and started reading, it was like water on dry ground. I soaked it up and realized how thirsty I was for the water that he alone can give. Once I was replenished and kept on replenishing my hunger for Jesus, I had a much better perspective on the uncontrollable, God sent a person into my life for a brief moment who helped me gain some needed insight, and I could put the uncontrollable situation behind me and move on.

Jesus has never moved away from you. If there is a distance between you and him, it's because you've moved away. That's one thing you can control—so move back close to him.

Our Thoughts

Paul wrote to the Corinthians, "We demolish arguments and every pretension that sets itself up against the knowledge of God, and we take captive every thought to make it obedient to Christ" (2 Cor 10:5).

I cannot overemphasize the importance of learning to control your thoughts and bringing every thought into captivity. What does it mean to make every thought obedient to Christ? I think of it this way: Would I want Jesus to hear what I'm thinking? Would I say it out loud to Jesus? If not, then I shouldn't be thinking it. After all, he knows all my thoughts anyway.

If you tend to brood on and think about the wrong things, imagine the worst, dwell on the negatives, and allow your thoughts to be controlled by the circumstances or by the wrong input you're pouring into your mind, you will never find victory over the uncontrollable nor will you know peace and contentment.

Follow Paul's instructions to the Philippians: "Whatever is true, whatever is noble, whatever is right, whatever is pure, whatever is lovely, whatever is admirable—if anything is excellent or praiseworthy—think about such things" (Phil 4:8).

Our Tongues

Another thing we can control is our tongues. Oops—that gets a little close to home, doesn't it? James tells us that when we control our tongues, we are able to control our whole personality (see Jas 3:2).

So much damage is done every day because tongues are out of control. Just think back over the past week: What words did you say that you wish you had not said? You didn't have to say them, but you did. They just came out before you knew it, and once they were said, they could not be unsaid. Oh, how we need to get control of our tongues and the words that we say. Relationships would improve immensely if we simply controlled our tongues.

That's something to pray about daily. I pray several scriptures into my life concerning the tongue, including Psalm 141:3: "Set a guard over my mouth, O Lord; keep watch over the door of my lips."

Our Attitudes

Attitude is always a choice. We covered that in detail in chapter one. Remember, if you've been shifting blame a lot lately, maybe you need to ask God to give you a new attitude. David prayed: "Create in me a clean heart, O God; and renew a right spirit [attitude] within me" (Ps 51:10, KJV). And Paul wrote, "You were taught, with regard to your former way of life, to put off your old self, which is being corrupted by its deceitful desires; to be made new in the attitude of your minds; and to put on the new self, created to be like God in true righteousness and holiness" (Eph 4:22-24).

We can control out attitudes by putting away the old self and putting on the new. As believers, we have the Spirit of God within us, and the Holy Spirit would not have a rotten attitude. If we have one, it's because we are not putting on the new self and are not being "made new in the attitude of our minds." But we can be made new at any time on any day that we choose to allow God's Spirit to change our attitudes.

Our Integrity

We can control our integrity and our dependability. Do you perform in all areas with complete honesty? Are you known as a dependable person? As believers in the marketplace, it is extremely important for us to take this issue very seriously. So much damage has been done to the name of Christ because of Christians who talk the talk but don't walk the walk.

Recently Paula related that she had received a paycheck that was calculated incorrectly and overpaid her by about one thousand dollars. Like any of us, she was tempted to let it slide. She knew it would most likely never be caught.

But Paula was committed to integrity in her life, knowing that Jesus knew if nobody else did, and that was more important to her than anything else. So she went to her supervisor and reported the error. He was surprised at her honesty and very appreciative. That is a testimony he will never forget. What a great eternal investment she chose to make by her commitment to integrity.

Paula never seriously considered doing anything else, because long ago she made a decision to be honest in any situation, no matter what the cost. That's the way integrity has to be established.

You can't wait until you're tempted to decide what you will do. It is a commitment that has to be made beforehand and before God, and one we reconfirm often.

Some ways we can establish integrity on our jobs include:

- Don't take anything that does not belong to you, no matter how small. That includes pens and pads, telephone charges, and your company's time.
- Don't lie about anything. There is no such thing as a "white lie." God does not excuse our lying in little things any more than he does in big things.
- Don't make promises carelessly, and when you do make a promise, take that commitment very seriously. Make sure you follow through and do what you say you will do.
- Avoid sloppy or slipshod work. When we don't work up to the levels of excellence of which we are capable, we lack integrity.

While it is true that few people are truly committed to a life of total integrity, it is also true that the world takes notice of a person who has integrity. The impact of that personal testimony cannot be denied.

Coping With the Uncontrollable

Those are just a few of the things in our lives that are controllable. If you and I will spend our time and energy keeping just those things under control, we will have the strength and wisdom we need to deal with the uncontrollable things that clutter our lives.

Here's how it works: When I focus on controlling the controllable, it takes my focus off the uncontrollable. I don't have as much time to be frustrated by those uncontrollable things and people because I'm busy controlling the controllable.

Then, when I control the controllable, I don't waste energy and time on the useless activities involved with the uncontrollable. As we discussed in chapter one, in any given day we have a limited amount of emotional energy to spend. When we spend it on frustration over uncontrollable things or people, we end up emotionally and physically depleted, with no resources left for other things. You'll be amazed at how energized you will be when you focus on controlling the controllable, because you'll see encouraging results.

If you've been spinning your wheels over the uncontrollable, I want to encourage you to enter into the joy of letting go of the uncontrollable and focusing on controlling the controllable. You will discover incredible freedom, you'll be more productive, you won't be tired as much, you'll get along with people better, and most importantly, you'll be more and more like Jesus.

Jesus didn't fret and bother about the Pharisees and religious hypocrites who were always trying to kill him or at least make him look bad. He just kept focusing on doing the Father's will. He didn't get frustrated when other people made demands of him that were not in his life plan. He just did what his Father had sent him to do.

At the end of a brief career, Jesus could say, "I have brought you glory on earth by completing the work you gave me to do" (Jn 17:4). He glorified the Father by controlling the controllable and letting the uncontrollable go.

We will thrive on our jobs and in all other areas of our lives when we focus on controlling the controllable. We will glorify God when we learn to allow him to take care of those things we cannot control. The uncontrollable is tolerable and manageable when we are focused on the right things.

The following exercise will help you consider ways you can control the controllables in your life.

Controlling the Controllables

1. Identify the situations and people in your life right now that you would change if you could:
    - ☐ Spouse
    - ☐ Job
    - ☐ Child(ren)
    - ☐ Home
    - ☐ Income
    - ☐ Manager
    - ☐ Coworker(s)
    - ☐ Marital status
    - ☐ Other:_____

2. Why do you want to change these situations or people?

    _____

    _____

    _____

3. Which ones could you change if you tried hard enough?

    _____

    _____

    _____

4. Which ones can you not change no matter what you do?

    _____

    _____

    _____

5. Which of the following areas in your life are out of control?
    ☐ My tongue
    ☐ My eating habits
    ☐ My health
    ☐ My body's condition
    ☐ My dependability
    ☐ My time management
    ☐ My work habits
    ☐ My procrastination
    ☐ My attitude
    ☐ My thoughts
    ☐ Other: _____

6. Recognizing that all the things you identified in question 5 are controllable by you, what are you willing to do to bring them under control?

    _____
    _____
    _____
    _____